Contents

Meditation Now

Inner Peace through Inner Wisdom

by S. N. Goenka

A Collection Commemorating
Mr. Goenka's Tour of North America
April–August, 2002

Vipassana Research Publications • Onalaska, Washington

Vipassana Research Publications
an imprint of
Pariyatti Publishing
867 Larmon Road
Onalaska, WA 98570
www.pariyatti.org

———————————— ※ ————————————

Second printing 2003
Third printing 2009
Fourth printing 2015

ISBN-10: 1-928706-23-1 (print)
ISBN-13: 978-1-92870-623-6 (print)
ISBN-13: 978-1-93875-421-0 (PDF)
ISBN-13: 978-1-93875-435-7 (ePub)
ISBN-13: 978-1-93875-436-4 (Mobi)

Library of Congress Control Number: 2002105397

The publishers are grateful to the following for their help with this collection:

The publishers and editors of the *Vipaśyanā Patrikā* and of the Vipassana Research Institute for their translations and generous assistance in gathering the materials.

Alan AtKisson for his kind permission to print his interview with Mr. Goenka.

S. N. Goenka

A Teacher for the World

Mr. Satya Narayan Goenka, the foremost lay teacher of Vipassana meditation, was a student of the late Sayagyi U Ba Khin of Burma (Myanmar). The technique which Mr. Goenka teaches represents a tradition that is traced back to the Buddha. The Buddha never taught a sectarian religion; he taught Dhamma—the way to liberation—which is universal. In the same way, Mr. Goenka's approach is totally nonsectarian. For this reason his teaching has a profound appeal to people of all backgrounds, of every religion and no religion, from every part of the world.

From Businessman to Spiritual Teacher

Mr. Goenka was born in Mandalay, Myanmar, in 1924. He joined his family business in 1940 and rapidly became a pioneering industrialist, establishing several manufacturing corporations. He soon became a leading figure in Myanmar's large influential Indian community, and for many years headed such organizations as the Burma Marwari Chamber of Commerce and the Rangoon Chamber of Commerce & Industry. He often accompanied Union of Burma trade delegations on international tours as an advisor.

In 1956 Mr. Goenka took his first ten-day Vipassana course at the International Meditation Center in Rangoon, under the guidance of Sayagyi U Ba Khin. In 1964-1966 Mr. Goenka's businesses and industries were taken over when the newly installed military government of Myanmar nationalized all industry in the country. This gave him an opportunity to spend more time with his teacher for meditation and in-depth training, all the while remaining a devoted family man and father of six sons. After fourteen years practicing with his teacher, he was appointed a teacher of Vipassana himself and devoted his life to spreading the technique for the benefit of all humanity. Shortly thereafter he came to India and conducted his first ten-day meditation course in 1969. In India, a country still sharply divided by caste and religion, Vipassana has been widely and easily accepted because of its nonsectarian nature.

The Vipassana International Academy *(Dhamma Giri)* was established in 1974 in Igatpuri, near Bombay, India. Courses of ten days duration and longer are held there continuously. In 1979 Mr. Goenka began traveling abroad to introduce Vipassana in other countries of the world. He has personally taught tens of thousands of people in more than 400 ten-day courses in Asia, North America, Europe and Australasia.

In response to an ever-growing demand, he started training assistant teachers to conduct these ten-day residential courses on his behalf. To date, he has trained more than 700 assistant teachers who have, with the help of thousands of volunteers, held Vipassana courses in more than 90 countries, including the People's Republic of China, Iran, Muscat, the United Arab Emirates, South Africa, Zimbabwe, Mongolia, Russia, Serbia, Taiwan, Cambodia, Mexico and all the countries of South America. More than 80 centers devoted to the teaching of Vipassana have been established in 21 countries. Today more than 1,000 courses are held annually around the world. One of the unique aspects of these Vipassana courses is that they are offered free of any charge for board, lodging or tuition; the expenses are completely met by voluntary donations. Neither Mr. Goenka nor his assistants receive any financial gain from these courses.

A prolific writer and poet, Mr. Goenka composes in English, Hindi and Rajasthani, and his works have been translated into many languages. He has been invited to lecture by institutes as diverse as the Dharma Drum Mountain Monastery (of Ven. Sheng Yen) in Taiwan; the World Economic Forum in Davos, Switzerland, and the Millennium World Peace Summit at the United Nations where he stressed for the assembled spiritual leaders the overreaching importance of inner peace to effect real world peace.

Teaching for All Sections of Society: From Prisoners to Government Officials

Vipassana meditation has been taught to prison inmates and staff in many parts of India as well as the United States, Britain, New Zealand, Taiwan and Nepal. There are permanent Vipassana centers in two Indian prisons. More than 10,000 inmates have attended ten-day Vipassana courses in jails and prisons. One thousand prisoners participated in a ground-breaking ten-day course conducted by Mr. Goenka in Tihar Jail, Delhi, in April, 1994. What started in a dramatic way in Tihar has now spread all over India. Convinced of its positive effects the Government of India has recommended that every prison in the country should organize ten-day Vipassana courses for inmates. As a result hundreds of prisoners continue to participate in Vipassana retreats every month. In addition, thousands of police officers have also attended Vipassana courses at the meditation center at the Police Academy, Delhi, and at other centers in India.

Men and women from all walks of life successfully practice Vipassana. They include the highly educated and the illiterate, the wealthy and the impoverished, aristocrats and slum-dwellers, devout followers of every religion and followers of none, the powerful and the powerless, the elderly and the young. Courses have been organized for people with disabilities, including the blind and leprosy patients. Other programs have focused on school children, drug addicts, homeless children, college students and business executives.

   High level institutions in India, such as the governments of the states of Maharashtra, Andhra Pradesh and Madhya Pradesh; large corporations such as the Oil and Natural Gas Commission; leading research institutes such as the Bhabha Atomic Research Institute; and national training institutes such as the Indian Institute of Taxation—all encourage their employees to attend Vipassana courses as part of their ongoing job training.

Commitment to Peace

Mr. Goenka believes and teaches that for peace outside (among nations, among different communities) there must be peace inside. Individuals must learn the "art of living "in order to live peaceful lives. This is the heart of his teaching to people from different backgrounds. One important consequence of his work in India has been a subtle but telling influence on interreligious harmony. Thousands of Catholic priests, Buddhist monks, Jain ascetics, Hindu *sanyasis* and other religious leaders have come, and continue to come, to Vipassana courses. The universality of Vipassana—the core of the Buddha's teaching—is providing a way whereby ideological differences can be bridged and people of diverse backgrounds can experience deep benefits without fearing conversion.

   Mr. Goenka recently made history in India when he and a leading Hindu leader, HH Shankaracharya of Kanchi, met and together exhorted Hindus and Buddhists alike to forget past differences and live in harmony. After this initial meeting Mr. Goenka also met HH Shankaracharya of Sringeri and many other top Hindu leaders in an effort to establish harmonious relations between Hindu and Buddhist communities.

Despite this positive development, mere exhortations alone cannot bring about the much desired reconciliation and cooperative spirit. Only when individuals undertake to remove from within themselves the blocks to peace and harmony can peace begin to flower outside and affect society. For this reason Mr. Goenka has always emphasized that the practical application of meditation is what will enable human beings to achieve inner as well as outer peace.

Vipassana Meditation
and the Laws of Nature

An Interview with S.N. Goenka
by Alan AtKisson

Introduction: *I can't tell you anything about what Vipassana meditation feels like, because I've never done it. But while definitions are tricky, what we call "spirituality"—the reaching of human awareness and conduct toward "that truth which passeth all understanding"—seems basic to meeting the enormous challenges of our times.*

Which is why I accepted an invitation to interview S. N. Goenka during his 1992 visit to the Seattle area, where I was living at the time. Goenka—a leading teacher of the ancient Vipassana meditation technique—is not spiritual "leader" in the sense one usually means by the term, for he has no "followers." He would likely prefer to be described as a scientist who researches the relationship of mind, body, and matter via insight meditation, and teaches others how to do the same—directly, for themselves.

A former wealthy industrialist, born in Burma to parents of Indian descent, Goenka turned to Vipassana (which means "insight," as in "seeing into reality as it is") when nothing else could alleviate his severe migraine headaches. He was introduced to the practice—reputed to be the method of meditation originally taught by the Buddha, though Vipassana itself is not a sectarian movement—by senior Burmese government official and meditation master, Sayagyi U Ba Khin.

Goenka became a devoted practitioner of Vipassana, and in 1969, having given up his businesses in Burma, he moved to India to begin teaching the technique in the land where it originated.

Two decades later, there are Vipassana meditation centers throughout the world, and they attract people from all faiths.

Many things seem to distinguish Vipassana (as taught by Goenka) from other meditation techniques, including its insistence on receiving an initial ten-day training directly from a qualified teacher.

But more importantly, in an era when too many priests and gurus have been accused of sexual or financial misconduct, the Goenka-led Vipassana network seems beyond reproach. As Goenka explains below, no one is allowed to pay for training in Vipassana, and no teacher is permitted to earn money from teaching. The expenses of those who take the training courses are covered by donations of time and money from students who came before them and want to help spread the benefit of the practice.

The following is condensed from a lengthy interview conducted at the Northwest Vipassana Center in Onalaska, Washington, in the summer of 1991.

—*Alan AtKisson*

* * *

Question: *Many people today are embracing the idea that truths are multiple—that there are many different kinds of truth, that truth is something created by humans and that there is no one ultimate truth. Yet Vipassana, as I understand it, seems to point toward an understanding of truth as something absolute. From the perspective of Vipassana, what is truth?*

Goenkaji: You are quite correct when you say that, generally, human beings have created truth. Different people have different views. Human beings are intellectual beings, and at the level of intellect—reasoning, logic—someone will say, "Perhaps this is so. It appears to be so. This seems logical." Someone else will say, "No, this is not logical, that is logical." All those perceptions are at the intellectual level, and the intellect has its own limitation—it differs from person to person.

But there are basic laws of the nature: for example, fire burns. What does this have to do with intellect? It is simply the truth. If you put your hand in the fire, it burns. If it does not burn, it is not fire, though it may be something else. This is the law of nature, which can be experienced by one and all. It is not somebody's intellectual game—it is truth.

Vipassana meditation works with the actual truth, which can be experienced by one and all. Vipassana is not an intellectual game. It is also not an emotional or devotional game. This is another kind of truth that human beings create: "I have great devotion in Buddha, so whatever Buddha says is the truth." " I have great devotion for Jesus Christ," and I will say, "Whatever Jesus Christ said is truth." These are devotional games and they also vary from person to person.

So truths which are based on devotion, or truths which are based on intellect, will always differ. They cannot be the same. But truth based on actual experience will remain the same.

Vipassana gives importance to the actual experience. The truth experienced by each individual is the truth for that person.

Now there are levels of experience; one may not be able to experience a particular truth now. But as one goes deeper inside—experimenting, experimenting, and starts experiencing subtler things, then everyone will experience the same subtle reality at the deeper level. It is not that only a particular gifted person will experience it—the law of nature is the same law for everybody.

Anybody who puts a hand in fire gets burned. Fire won't discriminate for a Hindu or a Muslim or a Christian or a Jew. The defilements of the mind act the same way: if you generate anger, hatred, ill will, animosity, passion, fear, ego, worry, anxiety—any impurity in the mind—it will make *you* miserable, it will make everyone miserable. The result is the same for an Indian or a Russian, a European or an American. The law of the nature does not discriminate, does not favor. This is truth, truth eternal—for everybody, all the time, past, present and future.

Similarly, if the mind is free from these defilements—if one does not generate anger and the mind is free from negativity, if the mind is pure—one will notice that the mind becomes full of love, full of compassion and goodwill. These good qualities arise naturally in a pure mind. And when these wholesome qualities are in the mind, one naturally feels very peaceful, very harmonious. Again, this is a law of nature. Whether you are a Muslim or a Hindu or a Christian, makes no difference, white or black or yellow, makes no difference.

Purity of the mind makes us feel very happy, peaceful and harmonious. We may belong to any community, any religion, any sect or none at all. Vipassana is beyond all religions, beyond all sects, beyond all beliefs, beyond all dogmas or cults. It is a pure science of mind and matter— of how they interact, how they keep on influencing and being influenced by each other. This reality is not to be accepted at the intellectual level, not to be accepted at the devotional level; it has to be experienced by each individual.

Suppose I have never *experienced* the burning of fire. I may have understood it intellectually because others have said, "If you put your hand in fire, it will burn." But once I have actually put my hand on a fire, and I find that it burns, naturally I will keep my hand away from fire afterwards. In the same way, if we understand intellectually that all these negativities make us unhappy, this is an intellectual understanding. But when you go deep inside, you can experience this truth for yourself: "Look, anger has arisen, and I have become so agitated. Passion has arisen, I have become so agitated. When any impurity arises, I become so agitated, so irritated, so miserable." You are *experiencing* it. And when you experience it directly, the next time you will be more careful not to generate such negativity: "Look, this is like fire. If I generate anger, it burns.

This is not a sermon, there is no a devotion involved: it is a fact, a hard fact of the life. If you defile your mind nature, the law of nature, starts punishing you then and there. It won't wait until after death and take you to hell. You suffer the pangs of hell now. You become so miserable. Similarly if you keep your mind pure—full of love, compassion and goodwill—it starts giving the reward here and now. Look, your mind is pure, no negativity: you feel so peaceful, so happy. So simple.

That's all Vipassana is, just following the law of nature. And by practicing, practicing; experiencing, experiencing, one starts changing the behavior pattern of the mind.

To come out of misery and live a happy life—everyone wants this, but one doesn't know how to do it. By the practice of Vipassana you go to the depth of your mind—where the actual misery starts because of these negativities, where the actual happiness is experienced because of the absence of these negativities—and once you start experiencing these things for yourself, a change automatically happens in your mind. You live a better life. Everyone lives better life.

Question: *Is Vipassana a religion?*

Goenkaji: No. There is no cult or sect or religion involved in Vipassana. For example, people used to be under the impression that the world was flat. And Galileo said, "No, it is round and it rotates on its own axis." This was so even before Galileo; it was so at the time of Galileo; it was so afterwards. People simply started accepting it: "Yes, it's true, it's round, it's rotating." They didn't get converted to "Galileo-ism," they didn't become "Galileo-ists." Similarly, there is a law of gravity in nature. Newton discovered it. That doesn't mean he created a law; the law was always there. The law of relativity was there too; Einstein discovered it.

In the same way in Vipassana, there is no conversion to any religion or any sectarianism involved. An enlightened person discovers this law, that when we generate negativity nature punishes us. Everyone wants to be free of this misery, and look, nature has also given us a way. We can observe it. We can observe the mind and matter reactions going on inside, and we will find we are coming out of it. This is the truth, which was always there. This universal truth can be experienced by one and all, all can benefit from it. A Christian will continue to remain a Christian his whole life, a Hindu a Hindu, a Muslim a Muslim, Jew a Jew. But they will start living a better life.

This is all Vipassana wants. This is what attracted me to Vipassana. I came from a totally different tradition, but when I passed through one Vipassana course I found it is so scientific, so rational, so non-sectarian, universal, and so result-oriented. It gives results here and now: what more could anybody want? Nobody told me to become a Buddhist. My teacher said, "If you are a Hindu you remain a Hindu. I don't care."

Doing Vipassana is like doing physical exercises to keep your body healthy. Here is a mental exercise to keep the mind healthy, which is much more important. The body may be very healthy, and yet if your mind is not healthy, you can't keep your body healthy. It will become unhealthy.

So to me this mental exercise is so scientific, so non-sectarian, so rational, so universal, that everyone should take advantage of it. It is not a foreign cult which is being imposed on a particular community, nothing like that. People are afraid, I understand, because many gurus have come from India and tried to exploit the people in different ways, financially and socially. People are afraid when they see, "Oh, another meditation teacher has come. Well, he may talk very fine, but ultimately he will try to exploit us and make us his slaves or this or that, or we may lose our own religion and get converted." That fear is natural, I can understand.

Question: *How is the Vipassana organization set up to prevent the kinds of abuse—especially financial and sexual—that have plagued so many other spiritual organizations?*

Goenkaji: Financial abuse is impossible in this tradition, because anybody who teaches must have some other means of livelihood. This teaching can never become a profession or a means of livelihood for the teacher, or the assistants, or those who serve on courses. Anybody who gives any kind of assistance in this organization must have his or her own means of livelihood. So that nobody expects anything. And even if something is offered, they are not supposed to take it. They are giving this service because they have gotten so much from it—as in my case.

I got so much from this technique. I was a very rich, very angry person, and very unhappy. I had a lot of problems in my life. And this technique took me out of those problems as if I had a totally new birth. So, because I feel so happy with this technique, I feel like sharing with others, because I know people are miserable in the same ways I was.

Rich or poor, everyone is living an egoistic, self-centered life, generating negativities, becoming miserable. If this technique is given to these people, they will become happy. So one feels like sharing it.

In the same way, there are those who have learned from me—thousands of them around the world—who feel like sharing. Some cannot serve, cannot give time, so they donate money. That donation is not like a fee for what they received. What they got, they got for free. They donate so that others can learn this technique. You see, this technique is such that it can only be given in a residential course—people have to come and stay for ten days. So there are boarding, lodging, and other expenses. But we do not charge people for those expenses—there is not a trace of commercialism involved. So where does the money come from? It comes from old students, who may feel that, "I can't personally go and serve people directly. But I am comfortable in many ways, so I will give five dollars, or ten dollars, or five thousand dollars, according to my capacity." And this is how it works.

Now, there are other way of exploiting people: one is socially. Those who start teaching may try to keep people under their clutches, like slaves: "My guru says I must murder that fellow," or "Whatever you have in your house, bring it and donate it here." All such things are possible, if people become slaves. The Vipassana tradition is totally against that. Each individual is one's own master. There is no "gurudom" involved. You experience the practice yourself. If you find it is good for you, then accept it. Don't accept the word of a guru unless you have experienced the teaching and found it helpful to you and helpful to others.

A guru may say, "You are a very ordinary person, I am such a wise, enlightened person, so whatever I say, you must accept." That is totally prohibited in Vipassana. Each individual has to enlighten oneself, and then only should one accept the truth—not because the teacher says so. Not because the Buddha said so. Not because the Christ said so. Not because the scriptures said so. You experience, yourself, the truth, and you find that, "Yes, it is good for me, good for others." *Then* you accept it.

Now with regard to sex, we have seen—and it is a very sorry state—that some people who are teaching spirituality (not all, but many of them) have had sexual relations with their own students. The whole teaching of Vipassana goes completely against that, because when a teacher gives the technique, gives Dhamma to anyone, then this person becomes like a son or a daughter of the teacher. A teacher must have that much love and that type of love and compassion, like the love of a father or a mother. How can one think of such madness as having sexual relations with one's students? Such a person is not fit to teach Dhamma. His mind is so full of passion, lust, impurity. How can he or she teach this—a technique for ridding the mind of impurities? Such a person is not allowed to become a full teacher. One is given the responsibility to teach only when one has developed to a stage where the mind is reasonably pure, and where one cannot have even a thought of sexual relations with a student. All assistant teachers are trained to develop these qualities and if anyone is found to have committed this kind of misconduct he or she will immediately be deauthorized from assistant teaching.

Question: *You were speaking earlier of the laws of nature and, right now, many people are observing that nature itself is in trouble. Some are concerned that much of nature is, in fact, dying, and many parts of our natural world are experiencing great suffering. Many people feel a great urgency about responding to that suffering and sometimes they feel anger towards those people who are causing it. What do you recommend? How might they respond to the suffering that they see—both in nature and in human society—with equanimity?*

Goenkaji: There are two aspects to this problem. One aspect is polluting the whole natural atmosphere, for example by different kinds of chemicals which harm the vegetation, the life of animals, birds and so on. Of course, any sensible, wise person must stop such pollution. If nature gets polluted, nature's harm is secondary. We are getting harmed. If the whole atmosphere becomes poisonous, how can people, who have mainly made it poisonous, live a healthy life? They have to live in this atmosphere, and they are spoiling it. So it's not that they should be kind to nature—I would say, better be kind to themselves. We don't understand what we are doing. Nature may be polluted now and later on again may become fresh again—after, say, some hundreds of years. Meanwhile, what have we done to ourselves?

So people should think about themselves. I want everyone to be selfish, but selfish in a proper sense. Right now, people don't know where their real self-interest lies, and they harm themselves. People need to be compassionate toward themselves.

Chemical poisoning is one kind of pollution that is harming people. But another, bigger pollution, happens whenever our minds generate a defilement. That defilement is nothing but a vibration—an unhealthy vibration. It first it defiles the atmosphere within ourselves, and then it starts permeating the atmosphere around us. If I become angry, I am the first victim of my anger. I am the first person who is harmed by it. The second victim will be affected a little later, but first, *I'll* be harmed. Then, after I am harmed by this anger, the vibration that goes out from me pollutes the whole atmosphere around me. If there are more and more angry people, how can you expect people to live peacefully in that atmosphere? It's impossible.

In a family, if there is one angry person, all the family members will become very unhappy. And if all of them are angry, it is a hell. What sort of life is that? But this is what is happening! People forget that when they generate negativity they are not only harming others, they are harming themselves. But if they learn Vipassana, this technique which nature has given us, they can come out of this pollution. See how peacefully they live now, how harmoniously! They are giving peace and harmony to the atmosphere. Anybody who comes in contact with that atmosphere will start feeling peace and harmony.

So that pollution is, to me, is more dangerous. For ages we have been doing this. Saintly people who experience the truth, come and say, "Oh, no, don't do this." But still we do. Because we do not understand that we are harming ourselves.

It is the same for the external pollution—people should understand that they are harming ourselves. A factory owner who is polluting the atmosphere with chemical gasses is not only harming others, he is harming himself also, living in that atmosphere. He can't have a separate atmosphere for himself. But one who is polluting the atmosphere at the mental level is suffering much more. The moment he starts generating anger, he is its first victim, and becomes a very miserable person.

So the atmosphere outside us is bad, as you say, and something has to be done. But when you said that people become angry when they see the pollution, that is not helpful. They have started producing *another* pollution with their anger. Anger cannot solve the problem. You must have *compassion* for other people. They are ignorant, they don't know what they are doing. We have to be firm and very stern, and very strong in opposing them, but deep inside there must be only love and compassion, no hatred. Hatred and anger cannot solve any problem.

Question: *It strikes me that what you are saying is something that all political leaders should hear.*

Goenkaji: Well, it starts from there. Every good or bad thing starts from the top and percolates through the society. If these people remain bad, the whole society has to suffer, and can't get the truth. But if the leaders start realizing that they are more or less owning the destiny of the whole human society, then they should live a better life, a good life, which can give a good example to the people—an example not just of power, but purity. Purity is the greatest power. If they learn how to keep their minds pure, they won't pollute the atmosphere around. And if they start doing that, it will certainly be so helpful to the whole human nation.

Question: *You said Vipassana requires a ten-day residential course. But is it possible to learn Vipassana on one's own? Suppose one lives where there is no access to a Vipassana teacher?*

Goenkaji: I would very much like it if people could just listen to a few words about the technique, which is so simple. In about ten minutes I can explain what the technique is, and people can understand. They can tell you what they understand.

But we have tried this and it doesn't work. Because from birth, when we first opened our eyes and started looking outside, we have been giving all importance to things *outside*. Our whole life we have been extroverted. Now all of a sudden we want to change that habit and experience things *inside*. Just *saying* that doesn't work. We have to practice. One wishing to practice must be under a proper guide, who has himself practiced properly, and who can guide properly. And must be in an environment where there is least disturbance. You can't learn it in the normal "marketplace" environment with all the disturbances. Once you have learned then, yes, you go to live in the world outside, with all its distractions, and yet you can practice. But for learning the first time, the proper environment is essential.

I know it is so difficult for somebody to find ten days of life free, to leave all one's other responsibilities and come to learn this technique. But it is essential.

Question: *What would you say to the businessman or the doctor who says, "I can't give ten days of my life"?*

Goenkaji: The same thing happened to me—I was such a busy businessman, an industrialist. For me to give ten days was unthinkable. I was a very angry person, a very egoistic person, living an ego-centered life, hating others and feeling that "I am the wisest and most intelligent person, because at this young age I have so much money. All the others are useless, that's why they can't earn money, they can't be successful in life." That ego was so strong.

Intellectually, I started realizing that this was so—and that it was my own ego, my own impurity which was making me miserable. How to come out of it? I tried different ways. I practiced devotional songs and chanting, for years, but this didn't work. I tried at the intellectual level to understand all the scriptures, how all the negativities are so harmful and the positive feelings of the mind are so good.

I kept on thinking, thinking, thinking, thinking. As with the chanting and devotional practices, this worked for some time only, but again I felt the same misery.

Then I contacted a wise person, Sayagyi U Ba Khin, who became my teacher. He said, "All these are games of the conscious level of the mind, the surface level, whereas your habit pattern lies at the root level."

The root level is what we call the unconscious mind. It is very blind. It will not listen to any advice from the intellect. It will not listen to any advice. It will just keep on reacting. Whenever it feels something pleasant, it will react with craving, clinging. When it feels something unpleasant, it will react with aversion, hatred. That has become the habit pattern of this deepest level of the mind. And unless we change this deepest level, all other things that we are doing at the surface are only temporary. They cannot help. If the root is unhealthy, the whole tree is unhealthy.

So you must go to that root. If you don't make the whole journey from the surface level of your mind to the depth of your mind, how can you change your mind at the depth level? That requires something like a surgical operation of the mind—and that requires proper guidance, a proper environment, and some time. You don't just sit down, meditate, and immediately penetrate to the depth; it's not possible. You have to go layer by layer, layer by layer, and reach the place where the deep unconscious mind is blindly reacting, all the time reacting: anger, hatred, anger, hatred, craving, clinging. These are the habit patterns. You have to reach that stage, and it takes time.

So I understood. If I am sick, I have to go to a hospital. I can't help it. And that may take ten days, it may take ten months. I have to take these ten days and see what happens. And now, I find everybody is a sick person. Each one requires this particular treatment. Less or more, everyone requires it.

So ten days, initially, will look like too much time to spare. But once people pass through a course, they start saying, "These are the ten best days of my life, up till now, and, I feel, for the future also. They gave me a totally new life." So people don't waste their ten days. Once they pass through it, they feel it is wonderful.

Question: *Many people come to something like Vipassana because they feel they are suffering in some way. But what about the person who doesn't feel he or she is suffering, who feels quite happy and satisfied? What motivation would they have to do this work?*

Goenkaji: Generally speaking, we can say that Vipassana helps everyone. One may be at any level in life, but one cannot say "there is no room for any improvement in me." One may be a very peaceful person, one may be a very intelligent person, very wise, very successful. There may be no obvious miseries in one's life. And yet, if one starts Vipassana, one starts improving—one becomes a much better person than before. Experience has shown this.

But frequently, when somebody says "there's no misery in me," this is only a delusion. This person does not know how much agitation there is inside. One remains deluded, in this sensual pleasure, that sensual pleasure; this satisfaction, that satisfaction—this is only at the surface level. Deep, deep inside, there is so much dissatisfaction. So much discontent. So one must first realize that "I am a sick person," and then must realize, "this is the cause of my sickness." And then one must try to remove that cause, to come out of the sickness. So one must have at least this motivation—to become a better person than what I am.

Very successful business people have become better business people, very successful writers have become better writers, artists have become better artists—in every sphere, in whatever profession one is involved, we find this general improvement in the mundane field occurs after one has practiced Vipassana. Leave the supra-mundane aside for the moment—it doesn't matter. But in the mundane, worldly field, as you progress in Vipassana, you will get better results.

Question: *Let's turn back to the supra-mundane. What does the science of Vipassana teach about the supernatural or the paranormal?*

Goenkaji: There are many experiences one might have which will be what are called "supernatural," but we don't give importance to them. They are also natural; they are not unnatural. Nothing is extraordinary. But if one aims for some kind of supernatural experience, then the whole purpose of Vipassana is lost. The purpose of Vipassana is to purify the mind, to live a good life. You may experience some supernatural powers, and yet if your mind remains full of anger, hatred, ill will, animosity, then what's the use of this supernatural power? It will increase your ego all the more: "Look, I am now such a big yogi because I can do this thing the others cannot do." This is madness; it doesn't help. So we don't give importance to these experiences.

Such experiences do come. On the path, the mind gets purer and purer, and a pure mind becomes very powerful. But it is powerful in a positive way. An impure mind, by certain mental exercises, can also become powerful—but that is an impure mind. It will harm itself, it will harm others. So purity of the mind is the aim of Vipassana; power is secondary, a by-product.

Question: *I heard a famous person speak recently, someone who was obviously very insightful, very wise, very intelligent, very brilliant—but also, to my perception, very egoistic, in a way that seemed potentially dangerous to that person and to others. How do you recommend responding to a person like that?*

Goenkaji: You see, if you simply say to that person, "Look, you are a very wise person, but to me it seems that you are also an egoistic person," that won't help. This person will become more egoistic: "What do you know? You are a mad fellow. You don't know that I am free from ego." That's what this person will say.

The best thing is to try to purify oneself first. With a pure mind, whatever you say will be very effective. When the words come from a pious-minded person, even this full-of-ego person will start thinking, "Yes, perhaps this is correct. Now let me examine this. There must be something wrong in me."

But when you say, with any kind of anger or hatred, "Oh, this fellow talks as if he is a very wise person, but he's really a mad fellow"—when even the volition carries some hatred—the words will carry no meaning. No purpose will be served, because the vibration of anger or hatred will go with them. When you have hatred, that vibration of hatred will go and touch this person and he will become agitated; he won't like it. But if a vibration of love goes with the same words, you will find a big change happening.

Everyone who wants to help others to come out of misery, or come out of their defects, must first come out of that particular defect oneself. A lame person cannot support another lame person. A blind person cannot show the path to another blind person. Vipassana helps you first become a healthy person yourself, and then automatically you will start helping others to become healthy.

Question: *Is Vipassana the only way to that purity?*

Goenkaji: Well, what do you mean by the "only way"? We have no attachment to the word "Vipassana." What we say is, the only way to become a healthy person is to change the habit pattern of one's mind at the root level. And the root level of the mind is such that it remains constantly in contact with body sensations, day and night.

What we call the "unconscious mind" is day and night feel-ing sensations in the body and reacting to these sensations. If it feels pleasant sensation, it will start craving, clinging. If it feels unpleasant sensation, it will start hating, it will have aversion. That has become our mental habit pattern.

People say that we can change our mind by this tech-nique or that technique. And, to a certain extent, these techniques do work. But if these techniques ignore the sen-sations on the body, that means they are not going to the depth of the mind.

So you don't have to call it Vipassana—we have no attachment to this name. But people who work with the bodily sensations, training the mind not to react to the sensations, are working at the root level. This is the science, the law of nature I have been speaking about.

Mind and matter are completely interrelated at the depth level, and they keep reacting to each other. When anger is generated, something starts happening at the physical level. A biochemical reaction starts. When you generate anger, there is a secretion of a particular type of biochemistry, which starts flowing with the stream of blood. And because of that particular biochemistry which has started flowing, there is a very unpleasant sensation. That chemistry started because of anger. So naturally it is very unpleasant. And when this very unpleasant sensation is there, our deep unconscious mind starts reacting with more anger. The more anger, the more this particular flow of biochemical. More biochemical flow, more anger. A vicious circle has started. Vipassana helps us to interrupt that vicious cycle. A biochemical reaction starts; Vipassana teaches us to observe it. Without reacting, we just observe. This is pure science. If people don't want to call it Vipassana, they can call it by any other name, we don't mind. But we must work at the depth of the mind.

Question: *I read that you've said that Buddhism has lost what the Buddha taught, which is the Dhamma, the*

Vipassana technique. What is your opinion of the Christian tradition? Was Jesus teaching something similar?

Goenkaji: Every saintly person becomes a saintly person because he or she has done something to purify the mind. There is no magic, no miracle. Such things were imposed later on. A person is a good person because one has purified the mind. And to purify the mind one must go to the depth of the mind and take out the impurities. This is what Jesus kept teaching to people.

Now, in every tradition, whether Christian or Jewish or Hindu or Jain or Muslim, what we call the founders of these religions were saintly people. They were not interested in fighting others in the name of religion—that started only much later. They taught a way to purify the mind, and that was lost everywhere. Nobody is practicing this. One may call oneself a Buddhist, but one is not practicing the technique taught by Buddha. It is the same with Hindus, the same with Christians, the same everywhere.

Why do I say this? Because people come to the Vipassana technique from all communities, from all religions. A large number of Christian nuns and priests have come, hundreds of them, and they keep coming. And when they pass through this, they say, "Now we understand what Jesus Christ taught." They learn Vipassana, and they say "Now, through this practice, we understand. We did not properly understand the words of Christ." You see, Jesus was a practitioner. He was talking about his experience. And unless we have that experience, we can't understand him. The same thing is said by Muslims when they pass through Vipassana, the same thing by Hindus, the same thing by Buddhists. Truth is truth. If one remains at the intellectual level, as I said at the beginning, or devotional level, then the truth differs from person to person. But at the level of experience, the truth is always the same—it makes no difference who practices it.

Question: *We are, of course, working at the intellectual level here, which is inevitable for the moment. But could you explain more about the body being vibrational? And is one always responsible for the agitation in one's own body, or is one susceptible to the vibrations coming from someone else?*

Goenkaji: Whatever vibration comes from outside, it will certainly try to affect you. But if you are your own master inside, then your vibration will be so strong that you will start helping and purifying the vibration outside. If I am a weak person, anything will try to overpower me. If agitation is coming, and I am a weak person, I'll succumb to that. If I am a strong person, I don't mind any kind of thing coming my way—I generate my vibration, which is a vibration of love, compassion, goodwill, stability, equanimity, and I'm not harmed. So that's why we say in Vipassana that one hundred percent of the cause of our misery is within ourselves, not outside. One hundred percent of the cause of our happiness is within ourselves, not outside. We are our own masters. Develop that mastery of yourself and you will become a happy person.

Question: *Some people would feel that they might be giving up some of the joy in life to also be giving up the participation in that agitation.*

Goenkaji: No. Life will be so joyful! Say you have enjoyed a particular type of life, having this sensual pleasure, that sensual pleasure. You say this is very joyful. But once you experience the joy of a balanced and peaceful mind, and you compare the two, you will find there is no comparison. The difference is like the difference between light and darkness, it is so great. One feels so happy: "Look, I have come out of it." One does not become like a vegetable, with no emotion in one's life. No, one's life is full of joy, full of life. Life becomes so bright and so good, so life-full. It is not lifeless.

But to the person who has not experienced this, it looks like illusion—"Oh, such peace of mind is not possible. Enjoying things at the sensual level is more important." It's not that after learning Vipassana we will run away from the sensual pleasures—but there will be no attachment to them. If we miss it, we miss it—still we are happy. If we get it, we get it—still we are content. Ordinarily, when you miss it, you will feel so depressed. With this technique, that depression will go away, so that you really are happy.

Question: *Well, it may be an illusion, but I am certainly enjoying this interview.*

Goenkaji: Find ten days to learn this technique and you will enjoy the real joy.

Question: *Let me ask you about suffering. What about children who are in great physical pain? They have no control over their suffering.*

Goenkaji: Parents are responsible for the joy, happiness, or misery of the child, at the initial stage. They need to give them a good atmosphere. If the parents are agitated all the time, quarreling, feeling anger, hatred, this, that, then the whole atmosphere of the family is such that the child cannot experience what real happiness is.

At present, there are so many different kinds of exploitation going on, so people are hesitant about every kind of meditation, whatever it is. But in a few years time, when more and more people start experiencing it, then this will become a part of the life of the society. Now we have our schools, colleges, gymnasiums, hospitals—these are necessary for the society. In the same way Vipassana centers will become necessary for the society. The children will go to these centers—not necessarily for ten days. They will just start by observing their respiration for few minutes. It will become a part of their teaching in the school.

In India, there is a school period which is called P.T., "physical training." I say, why not also have "M.T.," a few minutes of mental training? Ten minutes is enough, and the whole day works much better. Some of the schools have started this and are getting very good results. This will become very popular; it is bound to happen. Some people take it as a religion, a cult, or a dogma, so naturally there is resentment and opposition. But Vipassana should only be taken as pure science, the science of mind and matter, and a pure exercise for the mind to keep it healthy. What could be the objection? And it is so result-oriented, because it starts giving results here and now. People will start accepting this.

There are always initial difficulties—when a Vipassana center is started, the neighbors might say, "Oh, who are these people, what are they going to do here?" But after one, two, three years, they find it is something so good, it helps them also. Some of them will come and participate, and the word will start spreading. It has happened this way at every center. The initial year, there is a little turmoil. The second and third year, the neighbors start cooperating. It's bound to spread.

Question: *Since there are still not very many centers, and so many people in the world who can't get to one, it must be difficult to choose where to make this training available. Most of the new centers are being created in the West. Is the strategy to have it spread first in the places where people already do have enough to eat and can take care of themselves in that way?*

Goenkaji: No. I don't say that only such people can come, because of my experience in India where there is so much of poverty. Any ordinary, intelligent person will understand that first the stomach must be filled. A person with an empty stomach, how can he meditate? But that person also needs Vipassana, as much as a very rich person. To me, they are equally miserable.

Now, for the person who does not get even enough to fill the stomach one time during the day, this is so difficult. If that person comes to a course, for those ten days, at least, he is worried less about food. That person gets free food, free lodging, everything required, much better than he gets in his hut outside. And then he learns Vipassana. Going back out, he is able to face his difficulties much better. Of course, he has difficulties. I say the rich person has got more difficulties, but people never understand that.

In India, 25% or 30% of the people coming to the Vipassana courses live below the poverty line. Even people who sometimes go all day without eating, they come. After the ten days, their family members come sometimes and thank us. This person may have no money, but whatever money he does earn, even a small amount, he spends on alcohol or gambling, because he thinks this is the only way to come out of misery: "If I have some alcohol, I will forget the misery; by gambling, I might earn more." So these two addictions are there even with the poorest people in India. After just one or two courses, they are freed from these unwholesome habits. Automatically. Nobody tells them, "Going back home, you should not take alcohol." Nobody tells them, "Going back home, don't gamble." All that addiction is addiction towards body sensations. And once they have learned to observe body sensations, they come out of these addictions.

Vipassana has easily freed people from their addiction to drugs or alcohol, because all addiction is to body sensation. It looks as if one is addicted to alcohol, but no—one is addicted to the sensation that is created by taking alcohol, and one wants that sensation again and again. One has to take something to generate that sensation. Now through Vipassana, one learns that when the sensation comes, one simply observes. I am not reacting, so my attachment to it goes away.

So those people who are so poor, they start getting benefited even at the material level. Whatever they earn they now use for their family, for themselves. They have started living a better life. Previously they were not earning because of their agitated mind, because of the alcohol, because of the gambling. Now their mind is steadier, and they start earning much more. Whatever work they do, they get better results. So their earning increases, and their expenditure goes down. Materially, they are becoming better. These results are happening everywhere.

If a rich person who is very self-centered practices Vipassana, the self-centered nature goes away. That person realizes, "All this money that I am earning or that I have, why is it for me alone? It has come from the society. Of course it should be used for my maintenance or the maintenance of those who depend on me. Certainly I am a householder, I am not a monk or a nun. But it should also be used for the society, for the good of others." This person was just exploiting the society by grabbing money, legally or illegally, while other people were suffering. Now this person becomes so generous, for the good of others, and comes out of suffering in that way. Because this person was himself suffering. When he comes out of it, his accumulation is used for the good of others—that is also natural law There is no magic to changing the society, no miracle required. Things have gone so bad, let them come out in a proper way. They will, because Vipassana has started creating results.

Question: *Is it possible to fail at Vipassana?*

Goenkaji: Yes—if you don't work as your guide asks you to work. For ten days you are to leave behind everything else that you are practicing. You come for ten days to learn a very particular technique, a unique technique, which has its own special features. It takes you to the depth of the mind. You start from the surface, and go to the depth—a surgical operation. In the past, you might have been doing some other kind of meditation, where verbalization was involved, or visualization, or some kind of devotional practice, or some intellectual game, or some imagination. If you want to do any or all of these things while doing Vipassana, there will be a conflict inside.

The whole Vipassana technique wants you to go to the depth of the mind and observe the natural vibrations that are happening there, from moment to moment. If you are creating certain vibrations by your intellectual thoughts, or by your emotion, or by some verbalization at the surface level of the mind, and you want to go to the depth, there is a conflict. So without condemning what you were doing in the past, the teacher will say, "Leave that aside, and give this technique a trial for ten days. After ten days, you are your own master—if you don't like it, throw it away. If you like it, accept it. But don't mix those two during these ten days." Very rarely, if somebody mixes things in that way, then there is difficulty.

But otherwise, there is no possibility of getting into difficulty. And there's no possibility of failure. When you say "failure" it means not getting anything. There is not a single case where somebody has said, "I didn't get anything." One may get less or one may get more, according to what effort one has given to the technique. But a definite result is assured, there is no question.

Question: *Do all sensations have a purpose, or are some experiences meaningless? In practicing Vipassana, do you find that everything that happens to us has a purpose, a meaning?*

Goenkaji: There is a purpose—but if you don't know what the purpose is, every sensation that arises is giving you this lesson: "Look, I am impermanent. I am coming to pass away." Don't get agitated because of it. Don't get overwhelmed because of it. You learn. Make this sensation into a tool, to change your habit pattern. In that way, all experiences are very purposeful.

If we don't know what the purpose is, then we get over-whelmed, and we keep on reacting, reacting. We make ourselves worse. This is our ignorance. The purpose of the vibration is good, to give us a warning. I am angry, and the vibration has started, because of that anger. That is a warning to me: "Look, don't be angry, otherwise you experience this, and this will multiply." Now, if I don't take any interest in that warning, I will harm myself. But a very good purpose is there, so you start observing it: "Well, look, a sensation has come because of my anger, now let me see how long it lasts." I have made it a tool to come out of my anger.

Question: *Is there anything you want to emphasize about Vipassana?*

Goenkaji: Vipassana is nothing but an art of living. It should not be mixed with any religion, any dogma, any philosophy, any belief. All should be left aside. Vipassana is a code of conduct, a pure way for living a good life, a healthy life. It is good for oneself, and good for others. If Vipassana is taken that way—and that's the proper way to understand Vipassana—it will be very helpful.

But if it is seen with a colored lens—"Look, another religion has come, this is Buddhism, or this or that"—then one loses. Vipassana does not lose anything, those who are practicing Vipassana don't lose anything—but those who have such colored lenses will lose. Vipassana should be taken as a science, a pure science of mind and matter which starts at a very apparent, gross level, but takes us to much deeper and subtler levels, even to a level which is pure mind and matter. That is the important thing, and it is a message for everybody. That's why it is not limited to any particular community, any particular religion, or any particular country. It is for all.

Question: *I've enjoyed reading the teaching stories in your books. Would you close this interview with a story?*

Goenkaji: There is a story about a saint, sitting at the bank of the river. He sees a scorpion floating by, and he knows the scorpion will drown in the water. He wants to save the scorpion, but he finds there is nothing to use to take it out. So because he is a saint, he puts his hand in the water, and takes it out. He has love and compassion for the scorpion.

But as he lifts it out, the scorpion stings him and injects him with poison, and again falls into the water. Again he helps the scorpion. Somebody who is watching says, "What are you doing? You know that the scorpion will sting you, and yet you keep on doing that." "This stinging is the habit pattern of the scorpion, and my habit pattern is to serve. Why should I change my habit pattern?"

The job of the Vipassana meditator is to serve, to help, whatever the repercussions may be. And the repercussions will, ultimately, always be good.

Hatred Is Never Appeased by Hatred

After the terrorist attacks of September 11, 2001, in the U.S., Goenkaji wrote the following message for publication in the Vipassana Newsletter.

The recent tragedy in New York and Washington has shaken us all. We grieve for all the victims of this tragedy. And we grieve for all those innocent people who now live in the shadow of fear in the aftermath of this tragedy.

When there is darkness, light is needed.

This horrifying act has brought to our attention the dark side of the modern age. It has also put to the test our courage to face this tragic situation. I am sure that each Vipassana meditator must have generated love and compassion for all the victims of this tragedy. We wish that the perpetrators come to their senses and not repeat such crimes. We condemn the crime but have only compassion for the perpetrators. We understand the Universal Law of Nature, as taught by Buddha, "Hatred does not cease by hatred; by love alone it ceases. This is an eternal law." This law has nothing to do with Christianity, Islam, Hinduism, Buddhism, Jainism, Judaism, Sikhism or any other "ism." All peace-loving people understand this. And who doesn't want peace? When millions around the world greet each other with *Salaam walekum*—"May peace be with you" they do so with the same love for peace. My teacher, Sayagyi U Ba Khin, used to say, "Purity of mind is the greatest common denominator of all religions." No one with a pure mind can indulge in such dastardly acts.

It will be another great tragedy if this incident creates sweeping aversion against a particular community. Criminals are always very few compared to the common people of a particular society. Dhamma does not preach to blame those who are innocent. Division of human society into the compartments of religion is against Dhamma. Dhamma never divides; it unites. This is the time for us to express solidarity with innumerable peace-loving Muslims and Arabs. The Buddha used to say that all good and bad qualities are found in all the classes of society. Let us remember that. Let not the cowardly act of a few affect our perception of an entire faith. Let us be peaceful in this hour of crisis. "Blessed are the peacemakers: for they shall be called sons of God"!

We know that all such acts are the product of hatred and ignorance. Therefore let us work towards removing these from everyone's minds. Let us all meditate together and practice loving kindness for all the victims of the recent tragedy in New York and Washington and for all the people of the world.

The Universal Message of Peace

Address by S. N. Goenka
to the Millennium World Peace Summit,
UN General Assembly Hall, United Nations, New York 29
August 2000

In late August of 2000, Goenkaji participated in the Millennium World Peace Summit, a gathering of 1000 of the world's religious and spiritual leaders. This address was delivered to the participants at a session in the General Assembly chambers at the United Nations, under the auspices of Secretary-General Kofi Annan. The purpose of the meeting was to promote tolerance, foster peace, and encourage interreligious dialogue. With the many different viewpoints represented, the potential for disagreement was strong. In his presentation to the delegates, Goenkaji tried to highlight what they, and all spiritual paths, have in common: the universal Dhamma. His remarks were received with repeated ovations.

Friends, leaders of the spiritual and religious world: This is a wonderful occasion, when we can all unite and serve humanity. Religion is religion only when it unites; when it divides us, it is nothing.

Much has been said here about conversion, both for and against. Far from being opposed to conversion, I am in favor of it—but not conversion from one organized religion to another. No, the conversion must be from misery to happiness. It must be from bondage to liberation. It must be from cruelty to compassion. That is the conversion needed today, and that is what this meeting should seek to bring about.

The ancient land of India gave a message of peace and harmony to the world, to all humanity, but it did more: it gave a method, a technique, for achieving peace and harmony. To me it seems that if we want peace in human society, we cannot ignore individuals. If there is no peace in the mind of the individual, I do not understand how there can be real peace in the world. If I have an agitated mind, always full of anger, hatred, illwill and animosity, how can I give peace to the world? I cannot because I have no peace myself. Enlightened persons have therefore said, "First find peace within yourself." One has to examine whether there is really peace within oneself. All the sages, saints, and seers of the world have advised, "Know thyself." That means not merely knowing at the intellectual level, or accepting at the emotional or devotional level, but realizing by experience at the actual level. When you experience the truth about yourself, within yourself, at the experiential level, the problems of life find their solution.

You start understanding the universal law, the law of nature—or, if you prefer, the law of God Almighty. This law is applicable to one and all: When I generate anger, hatred, illwill, or animosity, I am the first victim of my anger. I am the first victim of the hatred or animosity that I have generated within. First I harm myself, and only afterwards do I start harming others. This is the law of nature. If I observe within myself, I find that as soon as any negativity arises in the mind, there is a physical reaction: my body becomes hot and starts burning; there are palpitations and tension; I am miserable. And when I generate negativity in me and become miserable, I do not keep the misery limited to myself; instead I throw it on to others. I make the entire atmosphere around me so tense that anyone who comes into contact with me also becomes miserable. Although I talk of peace and happiness, more important than words is what is happening within me. And if my mind is free of negativity, again the law starts working. The moment there is no negativity in the mind, nature—or God Almighty—starts rewarding me: I feel peaceful. This too I can observe within myself.

Whatever one's religion, or tradition, or country, when one breaks the law of nature and generates negativity in the mind, one is bound to suffer. Nature itself provides the punishment. Those who break nature's laws start feeling the misery of hellfire within, here and now. The seed they sow now is a seed of hellfire, and what awaits them after death is nothing but hellfire. Similarly by the law of nature, if I keep my mind pure, full of love and compassion, I enjoy the kingdom of heaven within here and now. And the seed that I sow will have as its fruit the kingdom of heaven after death. It makes no difference whether I call myself a Hindu, a Muslim, a Christian or a Jain: a human being is a human being; the human mind is the human mind.

The conversion that is needed is from impurity of mind to purity of mind. And this conversion changes people in wonderful ways. It is no magic or miracle; this is a pure science of observing the interaction of mind and matter within. One examines how the mind keeps influencing the material body, and how the body influences the mind. Through patient observation, the law of nature becomes so clear: whenever one generates mental negativity, one starts suffering; and whenever one is free from negativity, one enjoys peace and harmony. This technique of self-observation can be practiced by one and all.

Taught in ancient times by the Enlightened One in India, the technique spread around the world. And still today, people from different communities, traditions and religions come and learn this technique, to obtain the same benefit. They may continue to call themselves Hindu, Buddhist, Muslim, or Christian. These labels make no difference; a human being is a human being. The difference is that through their practice they become truly spiritual people, full of love and compassion. What they are doing is good for themselves and for all others. When someone generates peace in the mind, the entire atmosphere around that person is permeated with the vibration of peace, and anyone who encounters that person also starts enjoying peace. This mental change is the real conversion that is required. No other conversion has meaning.

Permit me to read you a benevolent message from India to the world. Inscribed in stone 2300 years ago, these are the words of the Emperor Ashoka the Great, an ideal ruler, explaining how to govern. He tells us, "One should not honor only one's own religion and condemn other faiths." This is an important message for our time. By condemning others and insisting that one's own tradition is the best, one creates difficulties for humanity. Ashoka continues, "Instead one should honor other religions for various reasons." Every religion worthy of the name has a wholesome essence of love, compassion and goodwill—every religion. We should give honor to the religion because of this essence. The outer form always differs; there will be so many variations in rites, rituals, ceremonies or beliefs. Let us not quarrel about all that, but instead give importance to the inner essence. As Ashoka says, "By so doing one helps one's own religion to grow, and also renders service to the religions of others. In acting otherwise, one digs the grave of one's own religion, and harms other religions as well."

This is a serious warning for us all. The message says, "Someone who honors his own religion and condemns other religions, may do so out of devotion to his religion thinking 'I will glorify my religion,' but his actions injure his own religion more gravely."

Finally Ashoka presents the message of the Universal Law, the message of Dharma: "Let all listen: Concord is good, not quarrelling. Let all be willing to listen to the doctrine professed by others." Instead of disagreeing and condemning, let us give importance to the essence of the teaching of every religion. And then there will be real peace, real harmony.

The Meaning of Happiness

The following is adapted from Goenkaji's address "Is This All There Is? The Meaning of Happiness" at the World Economic Forum, Davos, Switzerland, January, 2000.

Every person who is attending this forum is among a unique group of people on our planet. They are generally among the wealthiest, most powerful most accomplished individuals in the world. Even being invited to attend the World Economic Forum is recognition of the eminent status that each participant has reached among his or her peers. When someone has all the wealth, power and status that anyone could ever want, are they necessarily happy? Are all these accomplishments and the self-satisfaction they bring 'all there is'? Or is there some greater degree of happiness which it is possible to achieve?

Happiness is an ephemeral condition. It is rapidly fleeting; here one moment and gone the next. One day when all is going well with your business, your bank account and your family, there is happiness. But what happens when something unwanted happens? When something entirely out of your control happens to disturb your happiness and harmony?

Every person in the world, regardless of their power and position, will experience periods during which circumstances arise that are out of their control and not to their liking. It may be the discovery that you have a fatal disease; it may be the illness or death of a near and dear one; it may be a divorce or the discovery that a spouse is cheating on you. For people addicted to success in life, it may simply be a failure at something: a bad business decision, your company being acquired and the resultant loss of your job, losing a political election, someone else getting the promotion that you wanted, or your child running away from home or rebelling and rejecting all the values that you hold dear. Regardless of how much wealth, prestige and power you may have, such unwanted events and failures generally create great misery.

Next comes the question: how to deal with these periods of unhappiness, which spoil an otherwise ideal life? Such periods are bound to come in even the most charmed life. Do you behave in a balanced and equanimous manner or do you react with aversion towards the misery that you are experiencing? Do you crave for the return of your happiness? Moreover, when you becomes addicted to happiness and to everything always going the way you want, the misery when things do not go your way becomes even greater. In fact, it becomes unbearable. It often makes us resort to alcohol to cope with these situations of disappointment and depression, and to take sleeping pills in order to obtain the rest we need to keep going. All the while we tell the outside world and ourselves that we are sublimely happy because of our wealth, power and position.

I come from a business family and was an entrepreneur and businessman from a very early age. I built sugar mills, weaving mills and blanket factories and established import-export firms with offices all over the world. In the process, I made a lot of money. However, I also vividly remember how I reacted to events in my business and my personal life during those years. Every night, if I had failed to be successful in a business transaction during the day, I would lie awake for hours and try to figure out what had gone wrong and what I should do the next time. Even if I had accomplished a great success that day I would lie awake and relish my accomplishment. While I experienced success, this was neither happiness nor peace of mind. I found that peace was very closely related to happiness and I frequently had neither, regardless of my money and status as a leader in the community.

I remember a favorite poem related to this subject.

> It is easy enough to be pleasant;
> When life flows like a sweet song.
> But the man worthwhile,
> Is the one who can smile,
> When things go dead wrong.

How each one of us copes with these periods of things going 'dead wrong' is a major component of the 'meaning of happiness', regardless of our money, power and prestige.

It is a basic human need that everyone wants to live a happy life. For this, one has to experience real happiness. The so-called happiness that one experiences by having money, power, and indulging in sensual pleasures is not real happiness. It is very fragile, unstable and fleeting. For real happiness, for lasting stable happiness, one has to make a journey deep within oneself and get rid of all the unhappiness stored in the deeper levels of the mind. As long as there is misery at the depth of the mind all attempts to feel happy at the surface level of the mind prove futile.

This stock of unhappiness at the depth of the mind keeps on multiplying as long as one keeps generating negativities such as anger, hatred, ill will, and animosity. The law of nature is such that as soon as one generates negativity, unhappiness arises simultaneously. It is impossible to feel happy and peaceful when one is generating negativity in the mind. Peace and negativity cannot coexist just as light and darkness cannot coexist. There is a systematic scientific exercise developed by a great super-scientist of my ancient country by which one can explore the truth pertaining to the mind-body phenomenon at the experiential level. This technique is called Vipassana, which means observing the reality objectively, as it is.

The technique helps one to develop the faculty of feeling and understanding the interaction of mind and matter within one's own physical structure. The technique of Vipassana involves the basic law of nature that whenever any defilement arises in the mind, simultaneously, two things start happening at the physical level. One is that the breath loses its normal rhythm. I start breathing hard whenever a negativity arises in the mind. This is a very gross and apparent reality that everyone can experience. At the same time, at a subtler level, a biochemical reaction starts within the body: I experience a physical sensation on the body. Every defilement generates some sensation or the other in some part of the body.

This is a practical solution. An ordinary person cannot observe abstract defilements of the mind: abstract fear, anger or passion. But with proper training and practice, it is very easy to observe the respiration and the sensations, both of which are directly related to the mental defilements.

The respiration and the sensations will help in two ways. First, as soon as a defilement starts in the mind, the breath loses its normal rhythm. It will start shouting: 'Look, something has gone wrong!' Similarly, the sensations tell me: 'Something has gone wrong.' I must accept this. Then, having been warned, I start observing the respiration, the sensations, and I find that the defilement soon passes away.

This mental-physical phenomenon is like a coin with two sides. On the one side are the thoughts or emotions that arise in the mind. On the other side are the respiration and sensations in the body. Every thought or emotion, conscious or unconscious, every mental defilement manifests in the breath and sensation of that moment. Thus by observing the respiration or sensation, one is indirectly observing the mental defilement. Instead of running away from the problem, you are facing reality as it is. Then you find that the defilement loses its strength; it can no longer overpower you as it did in the past. If you persist, the defilement eventually disappears altogether and you remain peaceful and happy.

In this way, the technique of self-observation shows us reality in its two aspects: outside and inside. Previously, one always looked outside with open eyes, missing the inner truth. Human beings have always looked outside for the cause of their unhappiness. They have always blamed and tried to change the reality outside. Being ignorant of the inner reality, they never understood that the cause of suffering lies within, in their own blind reactions.

The more one practices this technique, the quicker one can come out of negativities. Gradually the mind becomes freed of defilements; it becomes pure. A pure mind is always full of love, detached love for all others; full of compassion for the failings and sufferings of others; full of joy at their success and happiness; full of equanimity in the face of any situation.

When one reaches this stage, then the entire pattern of one's life starts changing. It is no longer possible for one to do anything vocally or physically that will disturb the peace and happiness of others. Instead, the balanced mind not only becomes peaceful, it helps others to become peaceful also. The atmosphere surrounding such a person will become permeated with peace, harmony and real happiness, which also starts affecting others.

This direct experience of reality within oneself, this technique of self-observation, is called Vipassana and it is a simple direct way to leading a truly happy life.

There are different components of living a happy life. Several of these are relevant to the group of people attending the Forum. When you have all the money and possessions you could ever want, how can you really enjoy those blessings when millions of people in the world are

unsure of their next meal. While there is absolutely nothing wrong with earning money to provide for yourself,
your family and all those that depend upon you, you must
also give back to society. You are obtaining your wealth
from society, so you must give something back. The atti-
tude must be: 'I am earning for myself but I am also earning
for others.'

Another aspect of happiness in business is to be sure
that whatever you do to earn your money does not hurt or
harm others. This is a big responsibility. Money earned at
the expense of the peace and happiness of other fellow
human beings will never bring happiness to you. Real happiness is not possessions or accomplishments or wealth or
power. It is a state of inner being that comes from a pure
and peaceful mind. Vipassana is a tool that helps everyone
achieve that state.

Religion

*This is the second of three addresses given at the World Economic Forum,
Davos, Switzerland, January, 2000.*

Good that we are all here today to discuss various aspects of religion. Not this religion or that religion but
religion as such.

There are two significant aspects of religion, one of
which is the hard core of religion, the quintessence of religion, which is of utmost importance. This is to live a moral
life full of love, compassion, good will, and tolerance.

Every religion essentially preaches morality. This is the
greatest common denominator of all religions.

A moral life is a life where one abstains from all such
actions, physical or vocal, which disturb the peace and

harmony of other beings. A moral life is always free from negatives such as anger, hatred, illwill, and animosity.

A moral life is the true religious life where one lives in peace and harmony within oneself and generates nothing but peace and harmony towards others.

A true religious life is an "art of living," a moral code of conduct, and a happy harmonious healthy and wholesome life. A true religious life is always good for oneself, good for others, and good for the entire human society.

A true religious person is a pious person, a person with moral life, a person with a well-controlled and disciplined mind. A person with a pure heart always bubbling with love and compassion. A true religious person is an invaluable jewel of the human society. Such a true religious person can be from any country, community, any color, any sex, rich or poor, educated or uneducated. Every human being is capable of becoming a true religious person.

Living a life of morality with a well controlled, disciplined mind and with a pure heart full of love and compassion is not the monopoly of any one religion. It is for all. It transcends all sectarian barriers. It is always non-sectarian. It is always universal. It is always generic.

If people practice this quintessence of religion there is no reason for any conflict or confrontation among the people of the world regardless of their religion. Everyone in the human society can enjoy real peace, real harmony and real happiness by observing this quintessence of religion.

But then there is another aspect of religion. It is the outer shell of religion. It involves rites, rituals, ceremonies, etcetera, which are likely to turn into different cults. Each has its own different mythological and philosophical beliefs, each of which are likely to turn into dogmas, blind faith and blind beliefs.

In contrast to the uniformity of the inner hard core of morality this outer hard shell exhibits great diversity. Every organized, sectarian religion has its own rites, rituals, ceremonies, cults, beliefs and dogma. The followers of each organized, sectarian religion usually develop a tremendous amount of attachment to their own rites, rituals, faith and dogma as the only means of salvation. Such misguided persons may not have even a trace of morality, a trace of love, compassion and good will towards others and yet remain under the impression that they are religious persons because they have performed such and such rite or ritual or because they have full faith in a particular belief. They are actually deluding themselves and missing the nectar of the practice of the true essence of religion.

And then there is the worst part of this outer shell.

People with strong attachment to their own faith have the firm belief that the followers of all other organized sectarian religions are nonbelievers and therefore will never taste salvation. They are fully convinced that to convert others to their religion is a great meritorious deed and hence they apply various coercive m ethods.

Such blind faith of the followers of different organized religions is likely to turn into fanatic fundamentalism. It leads to controversies, contradictions, violent confrontations and even wars and bloodshed resulting in a tremendous amount of misery in the society, wiping away its peace and harmony. And all this is done in the name of religion. What a great misfortune for this human world.

When the outer shells of religion become so predominantly important the inner core of morality gets lost.

Sometimes people feel that there cannot be a religion without the hard outer shell, however undesirable it may be. But successful experiments were made in the past and are also being made even today where 100 percent importance is given to the inner core of morality, ignoring the outer shell as totally irrelevant. There exists a method to adopt this practice successfully called Vipassana meditation.

Anger

This is the final of three addresses given at the World Economic Forum, Davos, Switzerland, January, 2000.

What happens when someone is angry? The law of nature is such that one who generates anger is its first victim. One is bound to become miserable as one generates anger even though most of the time people do not realize that they are harming themselves by generating anger. Even if someone realizes this, the truth is that one is unable to keep oneself away from anger; to keep oneself free from anger. Now let us see why one becomes angry.

It is quite obvious that anger arises when something undesirable has happened, when someone has created an obstacle in the fulfillment of your desires, when someone has insulted you or when someone has expressed derogatory remarks about you while backbiting. All such reasons make one flare up in anger and are the apparent reasons for one to become angry. Now is it possible that someone can attain so much power that no one should say or do anything against him? This is certainly impossible. Even to the most powerful person in the world, undesirable things keep on happening and he or she is helpless to prevent it. Even if we can stop one person from insulting us or saying something against us there is no guarantee that another person will not start doing the same thing. While we cannot change the whole world according to our wishes, we can certainly change ourselves to get rid of the misery that one suffers because of generating anger. For this one has to seek a deeper reason for the anger within oneself rather than outside.

Let us understand within ourselves the real reason for generating anger. For example, let us understand from the standpoint of Vipassana the real reason which causes us to experience anger within ourselves. If you learn the art of observing the reality within yourself it will become so clear at the experiential level that the real reason for anger lies within and not outside.

As soon as one comes across some undesirable thing outside there is a sensation in the body. And because the object was undesirable the sensation is very unpleasant. It is only after feeling this unpleasant sensation that one re- acts with anger. If one learns how to observe bodily sensations equanimously without reacting to them one starts coming out of the old habit of flaring up in anger and harm- ing oneself. The practice of Vipassana helps one to develop the faculty of observing all the different kinds of sensations which one experiences on different parts of the body from time to time and remain equanimous by not reacting to them. The old habit had been that when you feel pleasant sensations you react with craving and clinging and when you feel unpleasant ones you react with anger and hatred. Vipassana teaches you to observe every sensation, both pleasant and unpleasant, objectively and remain equanimous with the understanding that every sensation has the quality of arising and passing away. No sensation remains eternally.

By practicing the observation of sensation equanimously again and again one changes the habit pattern of instant blind reaction to these sensations. Thus, in daily life when- ever one comes in contact with something undesirable one notices that an unpleasant sensation has arisen in the body and one starts observing it without flaring up in anger as before. Of course, it takes time to reach a stage where one is fully liberated from anger. But as one practices Vipassana more and more one notices that the period of rolling in anger is becoming shorter and shorter. Even if one is not able to feel the sensation immediately as it arises, maybe after a few minutes one starts realizing that by the blind re-action of anger one is making the unpleasant sensations even more intense, thereby making oneself even more miser-able. As soon as one realizes this fact one starts coming out of anger. With the practice of Vipassana this period of real-ization of misery pertaining to unpleasant sensation becomes shorter and shorter and a time comes when one realizes instantly the truth of the harm that one is causing to oneself by generating anger. This is the only way to lib-erate oneself from this mad habit of reacting with anger.

Of course there is a also a way that as soon as one real-izes that one has generated anger one may divert one's attention to some other object and by this technique one may feel that one is coming out of anger. However, it is actually only the surface part of the mind that has come out of anger. Deep inside one keeps on boiling in anger because you have not eradicated the anger but merely suppressed it. Vipassana teaches you not to run away from the reality but, rather, to face the reality and start objectively observing the anger in the mind and the unpleasant sensation in the body. By observing the reality of the unpleasant sensations in the body you are not diverting your attention somewhere else nor are you suppressing your anger to the deeper level of the mind. As you keep on observing the sensations equani-mously you will notice that the anger that has arisen naturally become weaker and weaker and ultimately passes away.

The fact is that there is a barrier between the smaller part of the mind, that is the surface of the mind, and the larger part of the mind, the so-called subconscious or half-conscious mind. This larger part of the mind at the deepest level is constantly in touch with the bodily sensations and has become a slave of the habit pattern of blind reaction to these sensations. Due to one reason or the other there are different kinds of sensations throughout the body at every moment. If the sensation is pleasant then the habit pattern is to react with clinging and craving and if it is unpleasant the habit pattern is to react with aversion and hatred. Because of the barrier between the small surface part of the mind and the rest of the mind the surface part is totally unaware of the fact that this constant reaction is taking place at the deeper level. Vipassana helps to break this barrier and the entire mental structure becomes very conscious. It feels the sensations from moment to moment and, with the understanding of the law of impermanence, remains equanimous. It is easy to train the surface level of the mind to remain equanimous at the level of intellectual understanding but this message of intellectual understanding does not reach the deeper level of the mind because of this barrier. When the barrier is broken by Vipassana the entire mind keeps on understanding the law of impermanence and the habit pattern of blind reaction at the deeper level starts changing. This is the best way to liberate yourself from the misery of anger.

The Art of Living

Everyone seeks peace and harmony, because these are what we lack in our lives. From time to time we all experience agitation, irritation, disharmony, suffering; and when we suffer from agitation, we do not keep this misery limited to ourselves. We keep distributing it to others as well. The agitation permeates the atmosphere around the miserable person. Everyone else who comes into contact with him becomes irritated, agitated. Certainly this is not the proper way to live.

One ought to live at peace within oneself, and at peace with others. After all, a human being is a social being. One has to live in society—to live and deal with others. How to live peacefully? How to remain harmonious within ourselves, and to maintain peace and harmony around us, so that others also can live peacefully and harmoniously?

When one is agitated, then, to come out of it one has to know the basic reason for the agitation, the cause of the suffering. If one investigates the problem, it soon becomes clear that whenever one starts generating any negativity or defilement in the mind, one is bound to become agitated. A negativity in the mind—a mental defilement or impurity—cannot coexist with peace and harmony.

How does one start generating negativity? Again investigating, it becomes clear. I become very unhappy when I find someone behaving in a way which I don't like, when I find something happening which I don't like. Unwanted things happen, and I create tension within myself. Wanted things do not happen, some obstacles come in the way, and again I create tension within myself; I start tying knots within myself. Throughout one's life, unwanted things keep happening, wanted things may or may not happen, and this process of reaction, of tying knots—Gordian knots—makes the entire mental and physical structure so tense, so full of negativity. Life becomes miserable.

Now one way to solve the problem is to arrange things such that nothing unwanted happens in my life, and that everything keeps on happening exactly as I desire. I must develop such a power—or somebody else must have the power and must come to my aid whenever I request it—that everything I want keeps happening. But this is not possible. There is no one in the world whose desires are always fulfilled, in whose life everything happens according to his wishes, without anything unwished-for happening. Things keep occurring that are contrary to our desires and wishes. So, in spite of these things which I don't like, how not to react blindly? How not to create tension? How to remain peaceful and harmonious?

In India as well as in other countries, wise saintly persons of the past studied this problem—the problem of human suffering—and they found a solution. If something unwanted happens and one starts to react by generating anger, fear, or any negativity, then as soon as possible one should divert one's attention to something else. For example, get up, take a glass of water, start drinking—your anger will not multiply; you'll be coming out of your anger. Or start counting: one, two, three, four. Or start repeating a word, a phrase, or perhaps some mantra. It becomes easy if you use the name of a deity or a saintly person in whom you have devotion. The mind is diverted, and to some extent you'll be out of the negativity, out of anger.

This solution was helpful; it worked. It still works. Practicing this, the mind feels free from agitation. In actuality, however, this solution works only at the conscious level. By diverting one's attention one in fact pushes the negativity deep into the unconscious, and at this level one continues to generate and multiply the same defilement. At the surface level there is a layer of peace and harmony, but in the depths of the mind is a sleeping volcano of suppressed negativity, which keeps erupting in violent explosions from time to time.

Other explorers of inner truth went still further in their search. By experiencing the reality of mind and matter within themselves, they recognized that diverting the attention is only running away from the problem. Escape is no solution; one must face the problem. Whenever a negativity arises in the mind, just observe it, face it. As soon as one starts observing any mental defilement, then it begins to lose all its strength. Slowly it withers away and is uprooted.

A good solution, avoiding both extremes of suppression and of free license. Keeping the negativity in the unconscious will not eradicate it, and allowing it to manifest in physical or vocal action will only create more problems. If one just observes, then the defilement passes away: one has eradicated that negativity, is free from that defilement.

This sounds wonderful, but is it really practical? When anger arises, it overpowers us so quickly that we don't even notice. Then, overpowered by anger, we commit certain actions which are harmful to us and to others. Later, when the anger has passed, we start crying and repenting, begging pardon from this or that person or god: "Oh, I made a mistake. Please excuse me!" Again the next time, in a similar situation, we react in the same way. All this repenting does not help at all.

The difficulty is that I am not aware when a defilement starts. It begins deep at the unconscious level of the mind, and by the time it reaches the conscious level, it has gained so much strength that it overwhelms me. I cannot observe it.

Then I must keep a private secretary with me, so that whenever anger starts, he says, "Look master! Anger is starting!" Since I don't know when this anger will start, I must have three private secretaries for three shifts, around the clock; or rather, four of them to give staggering holidays!

Suppose I can afford that, and the anger starts to arise. At once my secretary tells me, "Oh, master, look! Anger has started." Then the first thing I do is slap and abuse him: "You fool! Do you think you are paid to teach me?" I am so overpowered by anger that no good advice will help.

Suppose that wisdom prevails and I do not slap him. Instead I say, "Thank you very much. Now I must sit down and observe the anger." Is it possible? As soon as I close my eyes and try to observe the anger, immediately the object of anger comes into my mind, the person or incident because of which I became angry. Then I am not observing the anger. Rather, I am observing the external stimulus of the emotion. This will only multiply the anger. This is no solution. It is very difficult to observe any abstract negativity, abstract emotion, divorced from the external object which aroused it.

However, one who reached the ultimate truth in full enlightenment found a real solution. He discovered that whenever any defilement arises in the mind, simultaneously, two things start happening at the physical level. One is that the breath loses its normal rhythm. I start breathing hard whenever a negativity comes into the mind. This is one reality which everyone can experience, though it be very gross and apparent. At the same time, at a subtler level, some kind of biochemical reaction starts within the body— some sensation. Every defilement will generate one sensation or the other inside, in one or another part of the body.

This is a practical solution. An ordinary person cannot observe abstract defilements of the mind—abstract fear, anger or passion. But with proper training and practice, it is very easy to observe the respiration and the sensations, both of which are directly related to the mental defilements.

The respiration and the sensations will help me in two ways. First, they will be my private secretaries. As soon as a defilement starts in the mind, my breath will lose its normality. It will start shouting: "Look, something has gone wrong!" I cannot slap the breath; I have to accept the warning. Similarly, the sensations tell me: "Something has gone wrong." I must accept this. Then, having been warned, I start observing the respiration, the sensations, and I find very quickly that the defilement passes away.

This mental-physical phenomenon is like a coin with two sides. On the one side is whatever thoughts or emotions arise in the mind. On the other side are the respiration and sensation in the body. Any thought or emotion (whether conscious or unconscious), any mental defilement manifests in the breath and sensation of that moment. Thus by observing the respiration or sensation, I am indirectly observing the mental defilement. Instead of running away from the problem, I am facing the reality as it is. Then I will find that the defilement loses its strength; it can no longer overpower me as it did in the past. If I persist, the defilement eventually disappears altogether and I remain peaceful and happy.

In this way, the technique of self-observation shows us reality in its two aspects, outside and inside. Previously, one always looked with open eyes, missing the inner truth. I always looked outside for the cause of my unhappiness. I always blamed and tried to change the reality outside. Being ignorant of the inner reality, I never understood that the cause of suffering lies within, in my own blind reactions.

It is difficult to observe an abstract negativity when it arises. But now, by training, I can see the other side of the coin: I can be aware of the breathing and also of what is happening inside me. Whatever it is, the breath or any sensation, I learn to just observe it, without losing the balance of the mind. I stop multiplying my miseries. Instead, I allow the defilement to manifest and pass away.

The more one practices this technique, the more one will find how quickly he or she can come out of the negativity. Gradually the mind becomes freed of defilements; it becomes pure. A pure mind is always full of love, detached love for all others; full of compassion for the failings and sufferings of others; full of joy at their success and happiness; full of equanimity in the face of any situation.

When one reaches this stage, then the entire pattern of one's life starts changing. It is no longer possible for one to do anything vocally or physically which will disturb the peace and happiness of others. Instead, the balanced mind not only becomes peaceful in itself, it helps others to become peaceful also. The atmosphere surrounding such a person will become permeated with peace and harmony, and this will start affecting others too.

This is what the Buddha taught, an art of living. He never established or taught any religion, any "ism." He never instructed followers to practice any rites or rituals, any blind or empty formalities. Instead, he taught to just observe nature as it is, by observing the reality inside. Out of ignorance, one keeps reacting in a way which is harmful to oneself and to others. Then when wisdom arises—the wisdom of observing the reality as it is—one comes out of this blind reaction. When one ceases to react blindly, then one is capable of real action—action proceeding from a balanced, equanimous mind, a mind which sees and understands the truth. Such action can only be positive, creative, helpful to oneself and to others.

What is necessary, then, is to "know thyself"—advice which every wise person has given. One must know oneself not just at the intellectual level, at the level of ideas and theories. Nor does this mean to know oneself at the devotional or emotional level, simply accepting blindly what one has heard or read. Such knowledge is not enough.

Rather, one must know reality at the actual level. One must experience directly the reality of this mental-physical phenomenon. This alone is what will help us to come out of defilements, out of sufferings.

This direct experience of reality within one's own self, this technique of self-observation, is what is called Vipassana meditation. In the language of India in the time of the Buddha, *passanā* meant to look, to see with open eyes, in the ordinary way. But Vipassana is to observe things as they really are, not just as they seem to be. Apparent truth has to be penetrated, until one reaches the ultimate truth of the entire mental and physical structure. When one experiences this truth, then one learns to stop reacting blindly, to stop creating defilements. Naturally the old defilements are gradually eradicated. One comes out of all miseries, and experiences happiness.

There are three steps to the training which is given in a Vipassana course. First, one must abstain from any action, physical or vocal, which disturbs the peace and harmony of others. One cannot work to liberate oneself from defilements in the mind while at the same time continuing to perform deeds of body and speech which only multiply those defilements. Therefore a code of morality is the essential first step of the practice. One undertakes not to kill, not to steal, not to commit sexual misconduct, not to speak lies, and not to use intoxicants. By abstaining from such actions, one allows the mind to quiet down.

The next step is to develop some mastery over this wild mind, by training it to remain fixed on a single object, the breath. One tries to keep one's attention on the respiration for as long as possible. This is not a breathing exercise; one does not regulate the breath. Instead one observes the natural respiration as it is, as it comes in, as it goes out. In this way one further calms the mind, so that it is no longer over-powered by violent negativities. At the same time, one is concentrating the mind, making it sharp and penetrating, capable of the work of insight.

These first two steps of living a moral life and control-ling the mind are very necessary and beneficial in themselves. But they will lead to self-repression unless one takes the third step: purifying the mind of defilements, by developing insight into one's own nature. This, really, is Vipassana: experiencing one's own reality, through the sys-tematic and dispassionate observation of the ever-changing mind-matter phenomenon manifesting itself as sensations within oneself. This is the culmination of the teaching of the Buddha: self-purification through self-observation.

This can be practiced by one and all. The disease is not sectarian, therefore the remedy cannot be sectarian: it must be universal. Everyone faces the problem of suffering. When one suffers from anger, it is not Buddhist anger, Hindu an-ger, Christian anger. Anger is anger. Due to anger, when one becomes agitated, it is not a Christian agitation, or Hindu, or Buddhist agitation. The malady is universal. The remedy must also be universal.

Vipassana is such a remedy. No one will object to a code of living which respects the peace and harmony of others. No one will object to developing control of the mind. No one will object to developing insight into one's own reality, by which it is possible to free the mind of negativities. It is a universal path. It is not a cult. It is not a dogma. It is not blind faith.

Observing the reality as it is, by observing truth inside—this is knowing oneself at the actual, experiential level. And as one practices, one starts coming out of the misery of de-filements. From the gross, external apparent truth, one penetrates to the ultimate truth of mind and matter. Then one transcends that and experiences a truth which is beyond mind and matter, beyond time and space, beyond the conditioned field of relativity: the truth of total liberation from all defilements, all impurities, all suffering. Whatever name one gives this ultimate truth is irrelevant. It is the final goal of everyone.

May all of you experience this ultimate truth. May all people everywhere come out of their defilements, their misery. May they enjoy real happiness, real peace, real harmony.

How to Defend the Republic

The following is a translation of an article originally published in the September 1999 issue of the Vipaśyanā Patrikā.

It was the first year of the dispensation of the Dhamma. After attaining perfect enlightenment at Bodh Gaya and setting in motion the Wheel of Dhamma at Varanasi, the Buddha came to Rājagaha passing through Bodh Gaya on the way. Licchavī Mahāli, the commander of the Vajji republic, met the Buddha there. He benefited from his teaching and became his first Licchavī disciple. Inspired by him, many Licchavīs of Vesālī became devoted disciples of the Buddha within a few days.

Mahāli's skill in the art of warfare made the army of Vesālī a major force in the region. The Licchavīs had great respect for him. Unfortunately, he lost both his eyes. Therefore, they appointed him the chief military adviser and designated a brilliant Licchavī youth named Sīha as the commander of the army. At that time Sīha was a prominent disciple of another spiritual teacher. But when he saw that many Licchavīs of Vesālī had become the followers of the Buddha he came, after initial hesitation, to meet the Buddha out of curiosity. After talking to him, he was deeply influenced and became his devoted follower. Like Mahāli, Sīha fulfilled the responsibility of commanding the army with great skill and diligence even after becoming a follower of the Buddha. The Buddha did not teach his lay devotees to neglect their familial, social and official responsibilities. On the contrary, he would encourage them to gain more proficiency in them.

Once the Buddha came to Vesālī and stayed at the Sāraṃdada stupa. Many Licchavīs came to meet him and saluting him, they sat on one side. There was a constant threat of an attack upon Vesālī because the neighboring kingdoms were envious of its prosperity. The Buddha was aware of this. He also knew about the mutual antagonism between Magadha and Vesālī. Being born and raised in the Sākya republic, he understood the inherent advantages and disadvantages of a republic. Therefore, for the security of the Vajji republic, he gave seven practical instructions which would make them unassailable. These teachings were:

> 1. *Licchavīs! As long as the Vajjians maintain their unity and meet regularly they will remain invincible.*

The members of the state parliament of the Vajji republic (called *rājās*) would meet in the assembly hall regularly and discuss the security of the country. If they failed to assemble because of laziness, the enemies outside the border would get an opportunity to attack. On seeing that the *rājās* were not alert, these enemies would intrude into the country and loot the people. But when the *rājās* were alert, as soon as they were informed of any intrusion into the country, they would immediately send the army to rout the enemy. Then the intruders would understand that they would not be allowed to ravage the country. As a result they would scatter and flee.

> 2. *Licchavīs! As long as the Vajjians meet together in unity, rise in unity and perform their duties in unity, they will remain invincible.*

During times of danger, when the warning trumpet was sounded, every *rājā* would immediately come to the assembly hall. If any *rājā* was having his meal, he would leave it unfinished; if he was adorning himself with clothes and jewelry, he would come to the assembly hall at once, in whatever clothes he was wearing. There, everyone would sit together, and after deliberation and discussion, a unanimous decision would be taken. Thus, everyone would rise in unity. Thereafter whatever action had to be taken would be accomplished unitedly.

Everyone, he instructed, should be eager to protect the country. Whenever there is an announcement from any part of the country that the enemy has invaded any town or village and when the people are asked, "Who will go there and crush the enemy?" brave shouts of "Me first, me first" should echo throughout the country. During times of danger, all citizens should consider it their fundamental duty to defend the country. They should never fail to fulfil this duty.

> 3. *Licchavīs! As long as the Vajjians do not trans-gress their ancient principles of governance and system of justice, they will remain invincible.*

If any *rājā* arbitrarily increases taxes in his region or imposes fresh taxes, this will be a violation of the constitution and will cause discontent. Discontented people will not help during times of crisis.

Or if any *rājā* does not collect tax in his region out of favoritism, it will result in depletion of the state treasury. The army will not be able to procure necessary weapons. If the army does not get its salary on time, its strength will diminish.

There should never be any violation of the ancient penal code of the judiciary. According to the penal code, any person arrested on suspicion of having committed any crime has the right to appeal up to seven levels. He can appeal in turn to the minister of inquiry, the judicial magistrate, the chief magistrate, the jury, the commander, the crown prince and the king. If proved innocent in the course of any of these appeals, he is released. If he is ultimately proved to be guilty, he is punished. If he is punished in this way, the law breaker and his family as well as the people in the community will not have any grievance. But if he is punished without a fair trial and is not given an opportunity to appeal, it will be in violation of the judicial system, and people will become discontented. They will not give their full cooperation to resist the enemy in times of danger. If the government is run without the slightest violation of the judicial system, the people will be contented and will gladly help in the defense of the country.

> 4. Licchavīs! As long as the Vajjians revere, respect, venerate, and honor their elders and pay regard to their words, they will remain invincible.

If the respect for experienced elderly retired rājās of the country is maintained, if they are not ignored, then the country will continue to benefit from their long experience of governance and security of the state. The security of the republic can be strengthened with their experience about the way they united at the time of danger and saved the country; the way they deployed the army in the battlefield and destroyed the army formations of their enemies. If their advice is ignored, the country will be deprived of the benefit of their vast experience.

> 5. Licchavīs! As long as the Vajjians protect their women and do not abduct them, they will remain invincible.

The intoxication of power is extremely potent. If any rājā intoxicated by power harasses the womenfolk of others, their families will become unhappy and turn into enemies of the state. When the country is attacked, they will join the enemy and help in the destruction of the country to avenge the wrong done to them. If the rājās refrain from immorality, the security of the country will not be endangered.

> 6. Licchavīs! As long as the Vajjians venerate the objects of worship inside and outside their republic, and maintain monetary support to them, they will remain invincible.

There were many sects in those days too, with their own temples and places of worship. A wise nation should keep all the people happy and satisfied. They should not be harassed, compelling them to become enemies of the state. Their places of worship should be provided adequate protection. Whatever financial assistance they have been receiving from the state should never be stopped. Otherwise, not only will the deities of those places of worship become displeased, even more dangerous will be that their devotees will become enemies of the rulers and the state. They will join hands with the enemies invading the country. Therefore, for the security of the country, it is necessary to give suitable protection to these places of worship.

> 7. Licchavīs! As long as the Vajjians provide protection and support to saints and arahants, they will remain invincible.

Saints and arahants leave the country where they are not allowed to live peacefully, are disrespected, and even physically attacked. Moreover, saints and arahants from outside do not enter such a country. As a result, people are deprived of discourses on true Dhamma, and become immoral. Corruption increases and peace, prosperity and harmony are lost. The lack of virtuous people weakens the country. Therefore, the protection of saints and arahants is always necessary for the security of the country.

The Buddha stated that as long as the Vajjians followed these seven instructions, they would remain undefeated and the Vajji republic would prosper. Truly, following these instructions, the Vajjians remained invincible for a long time.

* * *

Years later, the scene of a tragic historic incident comes before us. The Buddha was about eighty years of age; forty-five years of his dispensation of Dhamma was about to be completed. Leaving Rājagaha, he set out on his last journey on foot. The king of Magadha, Ajātasattu sent his minister, Vassakāra to the Buddha with the news that Magadha was going to attack their enemies, the Licchavīs, soon. Without saying anything to Vassakāra, the Buddha asked Ānanda who was standing nearby, "Ānanda! Are the Vajjians following the seven instructions that I had given them years ago perfectly?

Ānanda said, "Yes Lord, they are following them perfectly."

Upon this, the Buddha said, "As long as the Vajjians follow these seven instructions, they will remain undefeated."

Vassakāra was skilled in the use of craft and deceit. He immediately understood that as long as the Vajjians remained united, they would truly remain unconquerable. He postponed the attack upon the Vajjians. The events that followed are the painful history of Vassakāra's deceit and the foolishness of the Vajjians, because of which their strong unity was completely destroyed. The dissension within them became so deep that they were not even able to unite to face the Magadhan army, let alone repulse their attack. The Licchavī republic became desolate forever. They forgot the beneficial teaching of the Buddha and sowed the seeds of their own destruction.

The universal teaching of the Buddha regarding the security of the republic is just as relevant today as it was then. The danger of destruction caused by internal discord is just as relevant today. Let the India of today learn a lesson from the Vajjians who forgot the teaching of the Buddha.

To preserve the strength of the republic for a long time, the seeds of dissension in the country should be removed. The issues that divide the country should be eliminated and the elements of unity should be strengthened. The country should not be divided because of sectarianism or casteism.

People of different sects can live together harmoniously in any country as long as they do not consider any sect as Dhamma. The difference between the two is clear. Different sects have different places of worship, different philosophical beliefs, different rites and rituals, as well as different clothes, festivals, traditions, food habits and fasts. Every sect may carry out its sectarian practices freely on the condition that the festivities of any sect do not offend the feelings of others. One should not consider any aspect of one's sect as Dhamma and generate blind devotional emotion. Sects may be different and may have different aspects; but Dhamma is always indivisible. Let the knowledge of the true nature of universal indivisible Dhamma spread among the people. Living a life of morality is Dhamma. One should not do any vocal or physical action that causes harm or injury to others and affects their peace and happiness. There is no monopoly of any sect on this; it is the Dhamma of all.

To live such a life, it is essential to gain mastery over the mind. Gaining mastery over the mind, controlling the mind is the Dhamma of all; it is not the monopoly of a particular sect. To gain mastery over the mind there should be a technique, which is acceptable to all sects.

Freeing and purifying the mind from the negativities of aversion and antagonism, one should fill it with love, affection and goodwill. This is the Dhamma of all; it is not the monopoly of any one sect. For this, one has to practice a technique which every sect can accept without any opposition.

The science that India gave to keep the body healthy in the form of *āsanas* (yoga postures) and *prāṇāyāma* (breathing exercises) is accepted world-wide because it is universal. It is not objectionable to any sect. In exactly the same way, rising above the sectarian walls of all religions, the universal Vipassana technique of ancient India, capable of controlling the mind and making it strong and healthy, has been accepted worldwide.

By taking the support of this beneficent universally acceptable technique of *sīla* (morality), *samādhi* (mastery of the mind), *paññā* (wisdom) and *mettā* (compassionate love), it is possible to establish an atmosphere of friendship and mutual love and affection. This will strengthen the unity of the republic.

Like the belief in sectarianism, the demon of belief in the caste system has also been dangerous to the security of the country in the past, it is dangerous today and will continue to be dangerous in the future. This is the lethal poison that has filled the blood vessels of the nation. The sooner it is removed, the better it is for the country's security and glory. The difference between high and low will persist in society, it cannot be eliminated; but it is necessary to eliminate the existing basis of discrimination. One should not be considered high or low just because of being born from the womb of one's mother. If a person commits unwholesome actions, if he is immoral, then he is wicked, unrighteous. He has little position in society; his status is low. Similarly, if he does wholesome deeds, is virtuous, then he is a good person, a saint. He has the respect of society; his status is high.

When the false belief in high and low status because of birth flourishes, Dhamma becomes weak. Then living a life of morality, that is, the practice of Dhamma is of no importance. If an immoral person gets a high position in society because of birth, morality becomes irrelevant. If because of birth, someone is considered to be of low status, there is no importance of morality for that person. If one is considered big or small, high or low, respectable or disrespectable in society on the basis of morality, then one who is low and dishonored today because he is immoral can become moral tomorrow and become high and respectable in society. When conduct instead of birth will be considered as the yardstick of high or low status in society, the progress of society will be abundant, the progress of the country will be abundant. The poison flowing through the blood vessels of the country since such a long time will turn into nectar.

May the practice of the nonsectarian universal technique of Vipassana that fills one with pure Dhamma lead to all-round development of the country; instead of mutual hatred and hostility, may love, affection and brotherhood increase. In this alone lies the security of the republic, in this alone lies the welfare and happiness of the country.

Awareness of Natural Respiration

The following has been translated and adapted from the sixth in a series of 44 Hindi discourses broadcast on Zee TV. It was originally published in the January 1999 issue of the Vipaśyanā Patrikā.

The goal of Vipassana meditation is to purify the mind completely by eradicating all mental impurities such as anger, hatred, passion, fear etc. For this, one must gain complete knowledge of the body, of the mind and of the mental impurities at the experiential level, which is done with the help of respiration.

If one wants to understand one's own physical and mental nature, one must use a pure object of concentration—natural, normal respiration. One should not try to regulate the breath or do any breathing exercise. Nor should one repeat any word or mantra or visualize any shape, form or imaginary object along with awareness of respiration. One should observe bare respiration, as it is.

When one observes respiration, one begins to understand the nature of the mind. One reality about the mind becomes very clear: the mind is very fleeting, very fickle. It wanders repeatedly from one object to another. Where does it wander? It wanders to so many objects. Even if one kept a diary, one would not be able to make a list of all the objects. But, if the meditator is attentive, he will see that the mind wanders in two areas only: either in the past or in the future. It recalls some past incident and starts to roll in thoughts of the past, "This had happened; this had not happened." Suddenly it may jump to the future and start rolling in thoughts of the future, "This must happen; this must not happen."

The meditator observes this present reality: he witnesses the nature of the mind objectively. Sometimes the mind wanders in the past, sometimes in the future. It never stays in the present. But one has to live in the present, not in the past. The past moment is gone forever. One cannot bring back that moment in return for all the wealth in the world. Similarly, one cannot live in the future. When the future becomes the present, only then can one live in it. So one can live neither in the past nor in the future. One has to live in the present, and yet, the mind constantly tries to escape into a past or future that is unattainable. One has not learned how to live; one has not learned the art of living.

Life can be really lived only in the present. Therefore, the first step of this technique is to develop awareness of a present reality: the breath entering or leaving the nostrils. The breath may pass through the left nostril, through the right nostril, or through both the nostrils simultaneously. One may find that after observing one or two breaths, the mind wanders away. One accepts this fact smilingly and again brings the mind back to respiration. The mind wanders again and again and one keeps returning to the awareness of respiration.

This does not mean that when one learns this technique one forgets the past completely or does not plan for the future. Oh no! After one learns the art of living in the present, one can easily recall things of the past whenever necessary and make suitable decisions about the future much more effectively.

One has to change the mind's habit of constantly wandering in the past or in the future. One has to train the mind to remain in the present. As one continues to meditate, one recognizes the tendency of the mind to constantly roll in thoughts. Of what type are these thoughts? The meditator sees that there are only two types of thoughts. Whether the mind wanders in the past or in the future, the thoughts that arise are either agreeable or disagreeable.

One is investigating the truth about oneself like a scientist, trying to understand the truth at the experiential level. One finds that whenever an agreeable thought arises in the mind about the past or the future, one feels very happy. And whenever a disagreeable thought arises in the mind about the past or the future, one feels very unhappy.

When an agreeable thought of the past or the future arises in the mind and it feels pleasant, one part of the mind starts reacting, "Oh, very good, I want more of it, I want more of it." And this habit—wanting, wanting—continues all the time. Similarly, we find that as soon as a disagreeable thought of the past or the future arises in the mind, a part of the mind starts reacting, "Oh, I don't want it, I do not want it. Let this never happen." And this habit—not wanting, not wanting—continues all the time. In India's ancient language, this habit of "wanting, wanting" was called *raga* (craving); and the habit of "not wanting, not wanting" was called *dosa* (aversion). One generates these thoughts of craving and aversion continuously in the mind. Agreeable or disagreeable thoughts, either of the past or of the future, cause pleasant or unpleasant feelings and result in craving or aversion continuously.

Sometimes a thought may arise in the mind and before it is completed, another thought arises. Before that thought is completed, a third thought arises. Thoughts arise without any sequence or meaning. Such mental behavior is commonly regarded as a sign of madness.

An example: A plate of food is served to a mad person who has been hungry since many days. He is happy because he was very hungry. He takes a morsel but before he can

eat, another thought arises in his mind—"I am in the bath-
room, I have come here to have a bath and this is a cake of
soap," and he starts rubbing the food on his body. Then
another thought arises—"This person standing before me
is my enemy, he has come to kill me. Before he kills me,
let me kill him. How can I kill him? These are hand-gre-
nades. If I throw them at him, he will die." So he throws all
the food away. Such a person is called mad.

A discerning meditator discovers that his mind is also
full of delusions, full of ignorance. In the ancient language,
this was called *moha* (ignorance). Because of this habit of
continuously generating craving, aversion or ignorance, the
mind is unhappy and agitated. At the surface level of the
mind, one tries to remain aware and to avoid generating
craving and aversion. At times, one may feel that the surface part of the mind has become very wise and does not
generate craving, aversion or ignorance any longer. But
this is a very small part of the mind. The larger part of the
mind, its deeper layers, is generating craving, aversion or
ignorance every moment. All mental impurities arise because of the stock of these impurities in the mind. The
deeper layers of the mind are unable to come out of this
strong habit pattern of craving, aversion, and ignorance.

During the whole day, there may be only a few moments when one is able to cut oneself off from the past as
well as the future and remain in the present. The mind is
fully concentrated on respiration, the truth of the present
moment. There is no delusion, no ignorance. One does
not generate craving for incoming breath or aversion towards outgoing breath. One simply observes the breath
entering and leaving the nostrils objectively without reacting to it. In such a moment, the mind is free from craving,
aversion, and delusion; it is completely pure. This moment
of purity at the conscious level has a strong impact on the
old impurities accumulated in the deeper levels of the mind.

The burning coals of craving, aversion and ignorance that one has accumulated within are smoldering. One has put thick layers of ash on them. The Buddha said that it is like burning coals covered by ash. It may seem that there is no fire under the layer of ash. But one is burning within because of these impurities. The contact of this internal burning with the coolness of this one moment of purity is like the contact of positive and negative forces. It produces an explosion, like the eruption of a volcano within. Some of the deep-rooted impurities may come to the surface and manifest as various physical or mental discomforts such as pain in the legs or in the head, or fear or agitation. What seems to be a problem is actually a sign of success in the meditation. When one cuts open an abscess, pus is bound to come to the surface. Similarly, the operation of the mind has started and some of the underlying pus has started to come out of the wound. Although the process is unpleasant, this is the only way to get rid of the pus, to remove the impurities. If one continues to work in the proper way, all these difficulties will gradually diminish.

When one pours a handful of water on a coal-stove to extinguish the fire, there is a reaction; there is a sound, "chung." When cold water is poured again, there is the sound of "chung" again. The hot stove will continue to make that sound until its temperature is the same as that of the water. Once this happens, it will not make any more sound when more water is poured on it. Similarly, when drops of this cool water of mental purity fall on the burning coals of the impurities within, it produces an explosion. Because of that, the meditator will feel restless. This is another reason why one is advised to learn the technique at a meditation center under the guidance of an experienced teacher.

If one works according to the instructions of an experienced guide at a meditation center, one learns to be equanimous in all situations. When one learns to keep the mind balanced, the mind becomes purer and purer. The purpose of meditation is to purify the mind. The development of a pure mind results in real happiness, real peace, real harmony, real liberation.

Walk the Path Yourself

The following has been translated and adapted from the seventh in a series of 44 Hindi discourses broadcast on Zee TV. It was originally published in the February 1999 issue of the Vipaśyanā Patrikā.

One who goes to a meditation center to learn Vipassana should clearly understand that the first step is to objectively observe the truth about one's own natural respiration.

No word should be added to the natural breath even as an oversight. One can concentrate the mind and make it calm by repeating any word. But the accumulation of defilements is blazing within, just as it did earlier. At any time, these sleeping volcanoes can erupt and overpower the mind and make one miserable.

Therefore, those who want to eradicate their defilements at the depth of the mind should not use any word. In other types of meditation, the use of a word has its own benefit. But it cannot eradicate the defilements at the depth of the mind.

One may repeat a word to concentrate the mind, just as a mother sings a lullaby to put her child to sleep. She keeps repeating the lullaby and the child falls asleep. In the same way, when a word is repeated, the mind will become concentrated on that. But this word becomes an obstacle in the objective observation of the truth in the present moment.

I can understand this obstacle because I myself used to meditate with the help of words. This has been confirmed by the experiences of others who have faced the same obstacles. A great saint from India, Kabir, said the same thing. As one continues meditating with the help of a word, an echo arises from within that is known as an *ajapa japa* (unchanted chant). This takes the form of a fine string and the string itself becomes an obstacle in the investigation of the truth of the universe within. Therefore, one is unable to attain the Ultimate Truth, beyond mind and matter. Kabir says,

> *Taga tuta, nabha mem vinasaga,*
> *sabad ju kaham samayi re.*

> The string has broken; it cannot remain in the universe within. How can the word that is so gross remain!

Therefore, one should not use any object that will become an obstacle to future progress on this path. One has to learn the truth about oneself at the experiential level: about one's body and mind and the interrelation between these two; and about the generation, multiplication and eradication of the mental defilements. One has to observe the truth as it is, just as it is. Then, one will keep progressing. The process of respiration is related to both: the body and the mind. By observing respiration objectively, the truth pertaining to both body and mind will become clearer and clearer.

There may be initial difficulties. One who wants to eradicate the defilements from the depth of the mind will have to face these difficulties. The mind is so restless, so unsteady, not only at the surface level but also at the depth. Like a monkey, this monkey-mind keeps jumping from one branch of a tree to another. As soon as it leaves one branch, it holds another. It is so agitated, so disturbed, so miserable. It is wild; it has to be tamed. And one has to do this work very patiently.

This work is similar to the task of taming a wild animal, like a wild buffalo or a wild elephant. To tame a wild animal a wise and experienced person works very patiently and persistently, because the wild animal does not become tame as soon as he starts the work. At home, one cannot do this work continuously. Also, one will not be able to do this work patiently in spite of the difficulties because there is no teacher to give proper guidance. But when one joins a course at a Vipassana center, one is able to work continuously and despite the difficulties, one keeps on making efforts to tame the mind.

It is not possible for one's mind to become totally concentrated and free of defilements as soon as one starts working. The mind will wander repeatedly. And when it wanders, it will be overcome by craving, overcome by aversion. And because of this, the meditator will become more and more agitated. "Oh, what kind of mind am I carrying! It is so full of craving, so full of aversion. It does not stay in the present at all. Our teacher says that one should live in the present but my mind does not stay in the present at all. It is so miserable." One has lost patience. One has lost equanimity. One has lost the balance of one's mind. How can the work proceed? One has to work very patiently. If the mind wanders, one accepts the present reality that it has wandered. If the mind is full of craving, one accepts the present reality that it is full of craving. One merely accepts: "At this moment, my mind is full of craving." or "At this moment, my mind is full of aversion." Thus, one keeps observing the state of the mind, as it is. One observes the natural respiration dispassionately, objectively, without any personal identification.

Something has happened at the physical or mental level and one understands, "I am observing" One starts the work in this way. As one progresses, one will reach a stage where this "I" will disappear, this "am observing" will also disappear. Something has happened and one understands, "It is being observed." There is no observer; there is only objective observation.

Influenced by Vipassana, Patanjali, an Indian sage who lived a few centuries after the Buddha, said, *"Draṣṭa dṛsīmatra"*—In seeing there should be only seeing. Later, this objective observation also ends, and bare awareness remains at the level of direct experience. This awareness is *sammā diṭṭhi*—right understanding, right knowledge. This eventually takes the Vipassana meditator to the final stage of full liberation.

Initially, one has to pass through many difficulties. When a wild buffalo or wild elephant enters any human habitation, it causes so much harm, so much destruction, so much panic. But after one has tamed the wild beast, by working very patiently, it is of such immense help. Its entire strength is utilized constructively.

The mind is more powerful than a thousand elephants. When it is destructive, it does more harm than a thousand wild elephants. The same mind, when tamed, will be of much more service than a thousand tamed elephants. A tamed mind will cause much happiness. But one has to work very patiently.

A meditator should also understand that "I have to do this work oneself. It is my responsibility." This is not out of egoism. Sometimes, because it was lost from India for such a long time, some people do not understand this technique of Vipassana properly and criticize it. They consider the idea of liberating themselves by removing their own defilements as egoistic. Oh no! This meditation technique will take one to a stage where the ego dissolves completely and there is only *anattā* (egolessness). The idea of "I," "mine," "my soul" will come to an end.

Liberating oneself is not egoism but a responsibility, just as one bathes every morning because one is responsible for keeping one's body clean. Who else will do it? Is one inflating the ego by bathing daily? Where is the question of inflating the ego? It is one's own responsibility. If the body becomes dirty, it becomes diseased. It has to be kept free from disease, therefore, one should clean it. Similarly, the mind has become impure. Who has made the mind impure? It is one's own responsibility. One did it out of ignorance because one did not have proper understanding. Now the job of cleaning it is one's own responsibility. One has to do it oneself; no one else can do it.

One often suffers from the delusion, "I am so helpless, I am so weak, how can I become liberated? Someone will have mercy on me. Someone will liberate me out of compassion." Such a deluded person should understand, "Why should the savior liberate me alone? Am I someone special? Just because I have become an expert at false praise, will the Almighty liberate me?" Why should the savior liberate you alone? The entire world is so miserable, and yet, he does not liberate anyone. It is clear that each person has to liberate oneself by removing one's own defilements. Each person has tied knots within, and these knots have to be untied by one's own efforts.

Someone full of compassion might show us the way. One who has reached the stage of liberation by walking on the path, a Buddha, will show the way. But one has to actually walk on this path oneself. One has to cover the entire path by walking step by step. At the start, someone might compassionately say, "Hold my hand and walk." Someone may walk alongside for a while but still one has to walk the path oneself. The sooner a person gets rid of the delusion that someone else will carry him or her on the shoulders to the final goal, the more beneficial it is for such a person.

Why would any unseen force generate defilements in the minds of all living beings and make them miserable? One has accumulated defilements oneself; one will have to remove the defilements oneself. Someone might lovingly show us the path.

As the Buddha says,

"Tumhe hi kiccaṃ ātappaṃ, akkhātāro tathāgatā."

You have to do your own work; Enlightened Ones only show the path.

The Buddha could show the path because he himself had walked the entire path and had reached the final goal. That is why he had become a *tathāgatā* (an enlightened person). Out of compassion for all suffering beings, he lovingly explained to people that it is their responsibility to walk on the path to liberation. The sooner a person understands that one has to walk on the path oneself, the more fortunate that person is. One who hopes that someone else will liberate him because he is so helpless will never walk on the path. One will have to make the effort oneself. There will be many difficulties and obstacles on the path. One may stumble and fall but one should get up and start walking again until one reaches the stage of liberation.

An incident:

The Buddha was dwelling at Savatthi, the capital of Kosala, the most densely populated city in the India of those days. Several monks and nuns as well as male and female lay people would come to his meditation center to listen to his discourses and to learn meditation. Some people came only to listen to the discourses but never put any of his teaching into practice. One such person arrived early one day and found the Buddha alone. He approached him and said, "Sir, I have a question that arises repeatedly in my mind. I am hesitant to ask when others are present. I am glad that you are alone today. With your permission, I will ask my question."

The Buddha replied, "There should not be any doubts on the path of Dhamma; have them clarified. What is your question?"

"Sir, I have been coming to your meditation center for many years and I have noticed that many people come to you. Some of them, I can see, have certainly reached the final stage and have become fully liberated. I can see that others have experienced a great change in their lives though they are not yet fully liberated. But sir, there are some people, including myself, who have not changed at all. They are just as they were earlier.

Why should this be, sir? People come to you, a great person, so powerful and compassionate. They take refuge in you and yet there is no change in them. Why don't you use all your power and compassion to liberate them all?"

The Buddha smiled. This is what he explained every day, but if someone did not want to understand, what could be done? He tried to explain again. He had different ways of explaining. Sometimes he would explain by counter-questioning.

"Where do you come from?"

"Savatthi, sir."

"Yes, but your facial features and speech show that you are not from this part of the country. You have come from some other region and settled here."

"You are right, sir. I am from the city of Rajagaha, the capital of the state of Magadha. I came and settled here in Savatthi a few years ago."

"Have you severed all connections with Rajagaha?"

"No sir. I still have relatives and friends there. I have business there. I visit Rajagaha many times every year and return to Savatthi."

"Having traveled the path from here to Rajagaha, certainly you must know the path very well?"

"Oh yes sir, I know it perfectly."

"And your friends, who know you well, must know that you are from Rajagaha and have settled here? They must also know that you often visit Rajagaha and that you know the path from here to Rajagaha very well?"

"Yes sir, all those who are close to me know that I am from Rajagaha and that I know the path to Rajagaha very well."

"Then it must happen that some of them ask you to explain the path from here to Rajagaha. Do you hide anything or do you explain the path to them clearly?"

"Sir, why should I hide it? I explain to them as clearly as I can: go towards the east from here and you will reach the city of Varanasi. Continue onward until you reach Gaya. Proceed further and you will reach Rajagaha."

"And do all these people to whom you explain the path so clearly reach Rajagaha?"

"How can that be sir? Only those who walk the entire path will reach Rajagaha."

"This is what I want to explain to you. People come to me knowing that this is someone who has walked the path from here to *nibbāna* and so knows it perfectly. They ask me about the path. Why should I hide it? I explain to them clearly:

"This is the path. On the way you will come across these stations; you will pass through these experiences. Proceed further and you will reach the stage of liberation, you will experience the Ultimate Truth.

"I explain the path very clearly. If someone is satisfied only with my explanation and bows down three times and says, '*Sadhu, sadhu, sadhu,* you have explained very well, sir.' but does not take a single step on the path, how will he reach the final goal?

"One who starts walking on the path and takes ten steps will be ten steps closer to the final goal. One who takes a hundred steps will be a hundred steps closer to the final goal. And one who takes all the steps on the path will reach the final goal. You have to walk on the path yourself."

All those who have started walking on the path of liberation, the path of pure Dhamma, have started walking on the path of total purification of the mind. They have started walking on the path of total liberation, the path that leads to real happiness, real peace, real harmony, real liberation. Those who walk on the path of pure Dhamma find real happiness, real peace, real harmony, real liberation from all the miseries of life.

The Importance of Daily Meditation

The following has been translated and adapted from a discourse by Goenkaji to about 5000 Vipassana practitioners at University Ground, Nagpur in October, 2000.

My dear Dhamma sons and Dhamma daughters, I am very happy that we have sat together and practiced pure Dhamma. Meditating together is of great importance. As the Buddha said:

> Happy is the arising of the Buddhas in the world.
> Happy is the teaching of pure Dhamma.
> Happy is the coming together of meditators.
> Happiness is meditating together.

Two thousand six hundred years ago, Gotama Buddha arose in this country and taught pure Dhamma resulting in great happiness for the world. People started living in accordance with this teaching. They started meditating together just as we have done today: there is no greater happiness than this. If one meditates alone, one becomes liberated from mental defilements and becomes truly happy. But when Dhamma brothers and sisters sit together and meditate in such large numbers, if someone's meditation is a little weak, it is strengthened because the meditation of others is strong and the entire atmosphere is charged with Dhamma vibrations. Whenever possible, meditators should have joint sitting at least once a week. If in the past week anyone's meditation has become weak, it is strengthened by the group meditation and he is able to face the vicissitudes of life for the whole week with renewed strength.

Every meditator has to develop the strength to face the ups and downs of life. For this, it is necessary to meditate one hour in the morning and evening daily, to meditate to-gether once a week, and to take a ten-day course at least once a year. Then we will keep progressing on the path of Dhamma. Householders face many difficulties, many ob-stacles. What to speak of householders, even those who have renounced the household life tell me that they are not able to meditate regularly. But we must not give up in spite of all difficulties; we must meditate daily, morning and evening.

We do physical exercise—yoga, jogging or walking—to keep the body healthy and strong. Otherwise, the body be-comes weak and diseased. In the same way, it is even more necessary to keep the mind healthy and strong. The mind is more important; one should not allow it to become weak or diseased. Vipassana is exercise of the mind. Meditating morn-ing and evening makes the mind strong and healthy; it is not a waste of time. We live in a complex and stressful world. If the mind is not strong, we lose the balance of the mind and become miserable. Those who do not know pure Dhamma, who have not learned this meditation, are unfortunate. But those who have received this benevolent teaching and are not using it are even more unfortunate. They have found such a priceless gem but have discarded it as if it is a useless pebble. What can be a greater misfortune?

It is a matter of great fortune to be born as a human being. Only a human being can become introverted and eradicate mental defilements from the depth of the mind. This work cannot be done by animals or birds or reptiles or insects or other lower beings. Even a human being cannot do this work if he does not know this technique. One gets a human birth, finds such a wonderful technique, learns to use it, benefits from it, and still discontinues the practice. What a misfortune! A bankrupt person finds a trea-sure. And he discards it and becomes bankrupt again. A hungry person gets delicious food. And he discards it and becomes hungry again. A sick person finds medicine. And he discards it and becomes sick again. Very unfortunate, indeed! One should not make this mistake.

Sometimes meditators come to me and say: "I have stopped meditating. What to do, I am so busy." It is a poor excuse. Do we not give food to the body three or four times a day? We do not say, "I am such a busy person, I don't have time for food today." This meditation that we do every morning and evening makes the mind strong. And a strong mind is more important than a strong body. If we forget this, we harm ourselves. We should never make this mistake. Even if there is too much work, we must do this exercise. Sometimes it is not possible to meditate at the same place at a fixed time. Though desirable, it is not a must. What is important is to meditate twice in twenty-four hours. In rare circumstances when one is not able to sit with closed eyes, one may meditate with open eyes; sitting with others with the mind directed inwards. We should not make an outward show of meditation; the others need not know that you are meditating. We may not be able to meditate as well as we could have done while sitting alone with closed eyes, but at least we have calmed and strengthened the mind a little. Without regular practice, the mind becomes weak. A weak mind makes us miserable because it reverts to its old behavior pattern of generating craving and aversion.

We have got human birth. We have come in contact with this wonderful Dhamma. We have developed faith in this technique because we have benefited from it, and yet, we have stopped meditating. Let us not be heedless. We are not doing anyone a favor by meditating twice a day. "Our teacher has told us, so we are doing it." You are not doing your teacher a favor; you are doing yourself a favor. This is such a great teaching. When one starts feeling sensations on the body, understand—the door of liberation has opened. A person who cannot feel sensation on the body is unfortunate; the door of liberation has not opened for him. And when one learns to remain equanimous to the sensations, not only has the door of liberation opened but one has entered it and has started walking on the path of liberation.

In Vipassana we experience different types of sensations on different parts of the body and maintain equanimity towards them. A wise meditator understands from experience how the practice benefits one in daily life. Every step taken on this path takes one closer and closer to the final goal. No effort is wasted; each effort bears fruit. Lack of awareness of sensations takes us on the path of misery. Blind reaction to them out of ignorance results in misery, deep misery— *dukkha-samudaya-gāminī-paṭipadā*. Awareness of sensations and equanimity towards them takes us on the path that leads to liberation from all suffering—*dukkha-nirodha-gāminī-paṭipadā*. If we experience sensations and react to them—react with craving to pleasant sensations and with aversion to unpleasant sensations—we are on the path of bondage. This is the teaching of the Buddha; this is the enlightenment of the Buddha.

At the time of death, some sensation will arise, and if we are not aware and react with aversion, we will go to lower planes of existence. But a good meditator who remains equanimous to these sensations at the time of death will go to a favorable plane. This is how we make our own future. Death can come at any time. We do not have an agreement with death that it should come only when we are ready. We are ready whenever it comes. This is not an ordinary technique. It is a priceless gem that can liberate us from the cycle of birth and death and can improve not only this life but also future lives ultimately leading to full liberation.

"But we do not have time. We have too much work." We squander an invaluable jewel by making these excuses. Whenever there is sorrow or despair or dullness in daily life due to any reason, this technique will help us. Just understand, "At this moment there is sorrow or despair or dullness in my mind," and start observing breath or sensations. The external reason is not important. The Buddha said:

> Sabbe dhammā vedanā-samosaraṇā

> Whatever arises in the mind is accompanied by sensation.

Whatever arises in the mind is called *dhamma*. A sensation arises on the body with whatever dhamma arises in the mind: this is the law of nature. The mind and the body are interrelated. When a defilement arises in the mind, some sensation will arise in the body. Whatever sensation arises in the body at that time is connected to the defilement in the mind. This is what the Buddha taught. One understands that there is a defilement in the mind and observes sensation in the body. One practices this thoroughly, not just once or twice, but again and again—every sensation is impermanent. So the defilement that is connected to it is also impermanent, how long will it last? We are observing sensations and also observing how long the defilement lasts. It becomes weak and ceases, like a thief who enters a house, and finding that the master of the house is awake, runs away. Take the example of anger. When anger arises due to any reason, one understands, "At this moment there is anger in the mind. Now let me observe what sensation has arisen in the body." It does not matter what is the cause of this anger. One is observing sensation and understanding that it is impermanent. This anger is also impermanent. It would have increased and overpowered one completely. Now it becomes weaker and weaker and passes away. It is such a great benefit. No matter what defilement arises, whether lust or egotism or envy or fear or anything else, one does not get overpowered by it. Now that we have learned this technique, we have learned the art of living. All that we have to do is to accept, "This defilement has arisen. Let me face this enemy. Let me see what is happening in my body. It is impermanent, *anicca, anicca.*" The enemy starts getting weaker and runs away. Defilements will keep coming throughout our entire life, sometimes for this reason, sometimes for that reason. When you become fully liberated from all defilements, you will become a fully liberated person, an *arahant*. At present, that stage is far away. Now in ordinary life, one has to face these difficulties. We have found a very effective weapon in the form of these sensations. No enemy will be able to overpower us for the whole life, how will it overpower us at the time of death? It cannot overpower us. We are the masters. This is the technique for becoming our own master.

We have learned the art of living. How can there be sorrow in our lives? Sorrow is caused by defilements, not by external events. An external event has occurred, we do not generate a defilement, we do not become miserable. An external event has occurred, we generate a defilement, we become miserable. We are responsible for our misery. Unfavorable external events will continue to occur and if we are strong and do not generate defilements, our lives will be filled with happiness and peace. We do not harm others; we help ourselves and help others. Every meditator should understand that one has to meditate regularly so that one is happy and peaceful for the whole life. All those who have come on the path of Vipassana should understand that they have received an invaluable jewel.

Awaken in Wisdom

These two articles about wisdom were originally published in the Hindi Vipaśhyanā Patrikā. They have been translated and slightly adapted.

Let us liberate ourselves from the bondage of ignorance. To become liberated from ignorance means to be liberated from the bondage of *dukkha* (suffering) in this life and *dukkha* resulting from the cycle of future births and deaths. It is ignorance that keeps us bound to *dukkha* in this life and in future lives.

What is ignorance? It is the state of dullness, heedlessness, unskillfulness. Because of ignorance, we keep generating new *saṅkhārās* (mental reactions) and keep defiling our minds with fresh negativities. We are barely aware of what we are doing: how we imprison ourselves with the bonds of craving, with the bonds of aversion; and how, in our ignorance, we tighten the knots of these bonds.

We can eradicate ignorance by remaining aware, alert, and attentive every moment. Then we will not allow new *saṅkhārās* to make deep impressions on our minds like lines chiseled on granite; we will not allow ourselves to be bound by the fetters of craving and aversion. This quality of attentiveness of mind, endowed with understanding, is called *paññā* (wisdom) and it eradicates ignorance at the roots.

To awaken this wisdom, and to get established in it, we practice Vipassana.

Yathaṃ care: when we walk, we walk with awareness.

Yatham titthe: when we stand, we stand with awareness.

Yatham acche: when we sit, we sit with awareness.

Yatham saye: when we lie down, we lie down with awareness.

Whether sleeping or awake, arising or sitting, in every state, we should remain aware and attentive every moment. No action of ours should ever be done without awareness.

> *Paccavekkhitvā paccavekkitvā kāyena kammam kātabba.*
>
> All body activities should be done with full awareness.
>
> *Paccavekkhitvā paccavekkhitvā vācāya kammam kātabba.*
>
> All vocal activities should be done with full awareness.
>
> *Paccavekkhitvā paccavekkitvā manasā kammam kātabba.*
>
> All mental activities should be done with full awareness.

Thus we should be heedful with regard to every physical, vocal, or mental action; we should examine every action.

At the same time, this awareness should be endowed with *paññā*. This means that, along with awareness, we should cultivate the experiential understanding of the three characteristics of *paññā*: that all phenomena, have the inherent characteristic of impermanence (*anicca*); that all phenomena which are impermanent give rise to suffering (*dukkha*); and that all such phenomena which are impermanent and give rise to *dukkha* are without essence—they cannot be "I" or "mine" or "my soul" (*anattā*).

Once this is understood at the experiential level, one realizes how meaningless it is to is react with craving or aversion, clinging or repugnance towards any phenomenon that arises. Instead, there should only be awareness and, at the same time, detachment towards every phenomenon. This is Vipassana. This is the experiential wisdom that shatters ignorance.

Meditators! In the destruction of ignorance alone is our welfare, our happiness, our liberation (*nibbāna*).

The Essence of Wisdom

What is wisdom? Wisdom means right understanding. Knowledge of the superficial apparent truth only is not true wisdom. In order to understand the ultimate truth we must penetrate apparent reality to its depths.

A child will see precious jewels only as attractive, colored pieces of stone. But an experienced jeweler evaluates the virtues and defects in each jewel with his expert vision in order to accurately estimate its value. In the same way, the wise do not conduct a mere superficial examination. Rather they go to the depths with penetrating wisdom and accurately perceive the underlying subtle truth in every situation. This ability to understand the complete truth accurately in every situation is wisdom.

There are three kinds of wisdom. The first, *suta-mayā paññā*, is the wisdom gained by hearing or reading the words of others. The second, *cintā-mayā paññā*, is intellectual wisdom: to test with one's reasoning and analyzing faculty whether the received wisdom is rational and logical.

It cannot be said that these two types of wisdom are absolutely useless. However, because they are borrowed

wisdom, usually the knowledge gained is merely intellectual and no lasting benefit is derived from it.

Bhāvanā-mayā paññā, the third kind of wisdom, is experiential wisdom It is wisdom manifested within ourselves,
based on our own experience of our body sensations. This
wisdom is based on direct experience and therefore is truly
beneficial.

To develop *bhāvanā-mayā paññā*, it is essential to practice *sīla* (moral conduct) and to develop right *samādhi*
(concentration). Only the mind established in right *samādhi*
can understand and realize the truth as it is. (*Yathā-bhūta
ñāṇa-dassana.*)

Samāhito yathābhūtaṃ pajānāti passati. One who has
developed right concentration, properly understands
reality as it is.

The ability to see things as they really are is called
Vipassana, meaning "to see things in a special way."
Ordinarily we tend to observe only the superficial apparent truth, like the child who sees only the superficial,
bright coloring and glitter of the jewels. To be able to
properly observe inner truth, we need the penetrating
expert vision of the jeweler—we need to see things in a special way. This special way of seeing is Vipassana; this is
bhāvanā-mayā paññā, the development of wisdom by the
practice of Vipassana.

It is easy to understand superficial reality but introspec-
tion is necessary to understand subtle inner truths. Directing
our attention inwards we must explore, observe, and understand the truth within.

To understand the truth within, we practice the four kinds
of awareness described by the Buddha in the
Mahāsatipaṭṭhāna Sutta. We practice *kayānupassanā*
(observation of the body) by observing the course of events
within the body with full attention. Observation of the

incoming and outgoing breath is part of *kayānupassanā*. Observation of the respiration leads to awareness of sensations on every part of the body.

Practicing diligently, we gradually begin to experience gross or subtle sensations on every part of the body. The sensations may be pleasant, unpleasant or neither-pleasant-nor-unpleasant. Observing these sensations with detachment, we practice *vedanānupassanā* (observation of sensations within the body). Observing the numerous kinds of mind (*citta*) that keep arising from time-to-time, we practice *cittānupassanā*. Observing the different contents of the mind, we practice *dhammānupassanā*.

We give more importance to *vedanānupassanā* because it is directly connected to the other three. *Vedanā* (sensation) is perceived by the mind, but it is experienced in the body. Every defilement in the mind is intimately connected with some sensation in the body. Therefore, when we strengthen *vedanānupassanā*, we automatically strengthen the other three.

In this way, through the practice of Vipassana based upon sensations, we can observe the true nature of the mind-body (*nāma-rūpa*) every moment. Gradually we develop the understanding that this body is merely a collection of subtle subatomic particles, which by nature constantly change, arising and passing away. These subatomic particles are made up of the four elements: earth, water, fire, and air.

The flow of the ever-changing body-stream and that of the mind-stream can be observed only with the help of penetrating, piercing *samādhi*. Observing the mind-body, we can experience its fundamental nature of impermanence (*anicca*) and suffering or unsatisfactoriness (*dukkha*) and in the process, its nature of egolessness (*anattā*) becomes clearer and clearer. We begin to realize that both the body-stream and mind-stream are substanceless, essenceless. There is nothing in this stream of mind and matter which is permanent, stable or constant, which can be called "I" or "mine," or which we can claim to control.

In this way, we begin to learn to observe the flow of *nāma-rūpa* with detachment, with impartially. The deeper the examination of the subtle sensations, the stronger our detachment. As long as there is attachment, we cannot observe the object of meditation objectively, as it is. Through the wisdom gained by practicing Vipassana, our attachment becomes weaker and weaker, and we are able to observe the object of meditation more and more objectively.

When one enters a dark house with a lantern, the darkness is dispelled; light illuminates the whole house and all objects in the house can be seen clearly. In the same way, the light of wisdom banishes the darkness of ignorance, and the eternal, noble truths are illuminated and are seen clearly.

Through continued practice, we experience the truth of *dukkha* at the deepest level—how this constantly dissatisfied and discontented mind is incessantly afflicted with the thirst of craving; how this thirst is never-ending—like a bottomless pit, it consumes all our efforts to fill it. We understand the misery of our attachment and clinging to our belief in an individual ego—how our attachment to this concept of self, to our cravings and opinions keep us incessantly preoccupied and miserable. When we understand *dukkha* and the root cause of *dukkha*, we also understand the Noble Path, which destroys all the cravings that cause *dukkha*, thereby leading to liberation from *dukkha*. As we progress on this path, we attain liberation from all suffering, *nibbāna*.

As our *paññā* grows stronger and stronger through the practice of Vipassana, this wisdom eradicates all delusions, illusions, false impressions, and ignorance. Reality becomes clear because false impressions are unable to stick in the mind. When *paññā* becomes strong, *sīla* becomes pure; the mind is purified of all defilements. And progressing on this beneficial path, we achieve the pure state of the *ariyas* (noble ones). We experience the joy of *nibbāna*.

The happiness gained through Vipassana is superior to any other happiness. Neither the enjoyment of gross sensual pleasures, nor that of subtle extra-sensual pleasures, leads to lasting happiness. When pleasure of any kind comes to an end, the result is sorrow. And because every situation is impermanent, it is bound to change, to come to an end. When a pleasurable experience comes to an end, the mind struggles to regain it. This craving brings misery. True happiness comes only from that which remains stable.

When we become used to observing with complete detachment, our faculty of observation can remain stable even if the objects of our observation keep changing. We do not become elated when we experience sensual or supra-mundane pleasures, nor do we cry when they pass away. In both situations we watch objectively, like a spectator watching a play. At the depths of the mind, as we observe the changing nature of even the most subtle sensations, right understanding arises about the profound truth of impermanence. We observe every changing situation with the same objective and impartial view. To see that which is apparent, that which is before our eyes, without any defilement in the mind—this is true happiness. This state has been called *ditta dhamma sukha vihāra* (the happy state of knowledge of truth).

Come, let us strengthen our *bhāvanā-mayā paññā* through the practice of Vipassana. Leaving behind the continuous struggle with cravings that cause such restlessness and discontentment, let us gain liberation from the bondage of craving. Becoming established in wisdom, let us gain liberation and attain real contentment, real happiness.

Work Out Your Own Salvation

The following article has been condensed from a discourse given by S. N. Goenka during a three-day Vipassana course for returning students.

At the surface, the mind plays so many games—thinking, imagining, dreaming, giving suggestions. But deep inside, the mind remains a prisoner of its own habit pattern, and the habit pattern of the deepest level of the mind is to feel sensations and react. If the sensations are pleasant, the mind reacts with craving; if they are unpleasant, it reacts with aversion.

The enlightenment of the Buddha was to go to the root of the problem. Unless we work at the root level, we will be dealing only with the intellect and only this part of the mind will be purified. As long as the roots of a tree are healthy they will provide healthy sap for the entire tree. So start working with the roots. This was the enlightenment of the Buddha.

When he gave Dhamma, the Noble Eightfold Path—the path of *sīla* (morality), *samādhi* (mastery over the mind) and *paññā* (experiential wisdom)—it was not to establish a cult, a dogma or a belief. Dhamma is a practical path. Those who walk on it can go to the deepest level and eradicate all their miseries.

Those who have really liberated themselves will understand that going to the depth of the mind—making a surgical operation of the mind—has to be done by oneself, by each individual. Someone can guide you with love and compassion; someone can help you in your journey on the path, but nobody can carry you on their shoulders and say: "I will take you to the final goal, just surrender to me; I will do everything."

You are responsible for your own bondage. You are responsible for making your mind impure, no one else. You are responsible for purifying your mind by breaking all the bondages. No one else can do that for you.

Continuity of practice is the secret of success. When it is said that you should be continuously aware, this means that you must be aware with wisdom of the sensations on the body, where you really experience things arising and passing away. The awareness of anicca is what purifies your mind, the awareness of the arising and passing away of these sensations.

Intellectualizing this truth will not help. You may understand: "Everything that arises sooner or later passes away. Anyone who takes birth sooner or later dies. This is anicca." You may understand this correctly but you are not experiencing it. Only your own personal experience will help you to purify your mind and liberate you from your miseries. The word for "experience" used in India at the time of Buddha was vedanā, feeling by experiencing, not just intellectualization. And this is possible only when a sensation is felt on the body.

Anicca must be experienced. If you are not experiencing it, it is merely a theory. And the Buddha was not interested in theories. Even before the Buddha, and at the time of the Buddha, there were teachers who taught that the entire universe is anicca; this was not new. What was new from the Buddha was the experience of anicca; and when you experience it within the framework of your own body, you have started working at the deepest level of your mind.

Two things are very important for those who walk on the path. The first is breaking the barrier that divides the conscious and the unconscious mind. But even if your conscious mind can now feel those sensations that were previously felt only by the deep unconscious part of your mind, that alone will not help you. The Buddha wanted you to take a second step: change the mind's habit of reacting at the deepest level.

Coming to the stage where you have started feeling sensations is a good first step, yet the habit pattern of reaction remains. When you feel an unpleasant sensation, if you keep reacting, "Oh, I must get rid of this," that will not help. If you start feeling a pleasant flow of very subtle vibrations throughout the body, and you react, "Ah, wonderful! This is what I was looking for. Now I've got it!," you have not understood Vipassana at all.

Vipassana is not a game of pleasure and pain. You have been reacting this way for your entire life, for countless lifetimes. Now in the name of Vipassana you have started making this habit pattern stronger. Every time you feel an unpleasant sensation you react with aversion; every time you feel a pleasant sensation you react with craving, in the same way as before. Vipassana has not helped you, because you have not practiced Vipassana in the right way.

Whenever you again make the mistake of reacting because of the old habit, see how quickly you can become aware of it: "Look, an unpleasant sensation and I am reacting with aversion; look, a pleasant sensation and I am reacting with craving. This is not Vipassana. This will not help me."

Understand that this is what you have to do. If you are not one hundred per cent successful, it does not matter. This will not harm you as long as you keep understanding and keep trying to change the old habit pattern. If you have started coming out of your prison for even a few moments, you are progressing.

This is what the Buddha wanted you to do: practice the Noble Eightfold Path. Practice *sīla* so that you can have the right type of samādhi. For those who keep breaking sīla, there is little hope that they will go to the deepest levels of reality. Sīla develops after you have some control over your mind, after you start understanding with paññā that breaking sīla is very harmful. Your paññā at the experiential level will help your samādhi. Your samādhi at the experiential level will help your sīla. Strong sīla will help your samādhi become strong. Strong samādhi will help your paññā become strong. Each of the three will start helping the other two and you will keep progressing, progressing on the path.

There were many techniques in India in those days, and also later on, practicing which meditators started feeling subtle vibrations throughout the body, when the solidity of the body had dissolved. The truth is that even the subtlest vibration one can experience is still a phenomenon in the field of mind and matter. It is arising, passing, arising, passing; still in the field of anicca, a field of constant change.

Some meditators of old tried to impose a philosophy on this subtle experience. Having reached the stage where they experienced nothing but vibrations, they postulated: "Throughout the universe, there is this subtle energy. This is God Almighty. I am experiencing this; I am with God Almighty. The entire universe is one. Every being is God. Why should I have any kind of preference or prejudice?" It is a very positive mental suggestion but it only helps at a superficial level.

The reality is that even this very subtle experience is still in the field of mind and matter; it is not the ultimate truth that is beyond mind and matter. All these suggestions, however positive they may be, cannot liberate anyone. You must be with reality: all vibrations are nothing but a flux, a flow. This realization removes the deep-rooted habit pattern of reacting to the sensations.

Whatever sensations you experience—pleasant, unpleasant or neutral—you should use them as tools. These sensations can become tools to liberate you from your misery, provided you understand the truth as it is. But these same sensations can also become tools that multiply your misery. Likes and dislikes should not cloud the issue. The reality is: sensations are arising and passing away; they are *anicca*. Pleasant, unpleasant or neutral—it makes no difference. When you start realizing the fact that even the most pleasant sensations you experience are *dukkha* (suffering), then you are coming nearer to liberation.

Understand why pleasant sensations are *dukkha*. Every time a pleasant sensation arises, you start relishing it. This habit of clinging to pleasant sensations has persisted for countless lifetimes, and it is because of this that you have aversion. Craving and aversion are two sides of the same coin. The stronger the craving, the stronger aversion is bound to be. Sooner or later every pleasant sensation turns into an unpleasant one, and every unpleasant sensation will turn into a pleasant one; this is the law of nature. If you start craving pleasant sensations, you are inviting misery.

The Buddha's teaching helps us to disintegrate the solidified intensity that keeps us from seeing the real truth. At the actual level, there are mere vibrations, nothing else. At the same time, there is solidity. For example, this wall is solid. This is a truth, an apparent truth. The ultimate truth is that what you call a wall is nothing but a mass of vibrating subatomic particles. We have to integrate both these truths through proper understanding.

Dhamma develops our understanding, so that we free ourselves from the habit of reacting and understand that craving is harming us, aversion is harming us. And then we become more realistic: "See, there is ultimate truth, but there is also apparent truth, which is also a truth."

The process of going to the depth of the mind to liberate yourself is done by you alone; but you must also be prepared to work with your family, with society as a whole.

The yardstick to measure whether love, compassion and goodwill are truly developing within you is whether these qualities are being exhibited toward the people around you.

The Buddha wanted us to be liberated at the deepest level of our minds. And that is possible only when three characteristics are realized: *anicca* (impermanence), *dukkha* (suffering) and *anatta* (egolessness). When the mind starts to become deconditioned, layer after layer becomes purified until the mind is totally unconditioned. Then purity becomes a way of life. You will not have to practice *mettā* (compassionate love) as you do now at the end of your one-hour sitting. Later, *mettā* just becomes a part of your life. All the time you will remain suffused with love, compassion and good will. This is the aim, the goal.

The path of liberation is the path of working at the deepest level of the mind. There is nothing wrong with giving good mental suggestions, but unless you change the blind habit of reacting at the deepest level, you are not liberated. Nobody is liberated unless the deepest level of the mind is changed. And the deepest level of the mind is constantly in contact with bodily sensations.

We have to divide, dissect and disintegrate the entire structure to understand how mind and matter are interrelated. If you work only with the mind and forget the body, you are not practicing the Buddha's teaching. If you work only with the body and forget the mind, again you are not understanding the Buddha properly.

Anything that arises in the mind turns into matter, into a sensation in the material field. This was the Buddha's discovery. People forgot this truth, which can only be understood through proper practice. The Buddha said, "*Sabbe dhammā vedanā samosaraṇā,*" anything that arises in the mind starts flowing as a sensation on the body.

The Buddha used the word *āsava*, which means flow or intoxication. Suppose you have generated anger. A biochemical flow starts, which generates very unpleasant sensations. Because of these unpleasant sensations, you start reacting with anger. As you generate anger, the flow becomes stronger. There are unpleasant sensations and, with them, a biochemical secretion. As you generate more anger, the flow becomes stronger.

In the same way, when passion or fear arises, a particular type of biochemical substance starts flowing in the blood. A vicious circle starts, which keeps repeating itself. There is a flow, an intoxication, at the depth of the mind. Out of ignorance, we become intoxicated by this particular biochemical flow. Although it makes us miserable, yet we become intoxicated: we want it again and again. So we keep on generating more and more anger, more and more passion, more and more fear. We become intoxicated by whatever impurity we generate in the mind. When we say that someone is addicted to alcohol or drugs, this is untrue. No one is addicted to alcohol or drugs. The actual truth is that one is addicted to the sensations that are produced by the alcohol or drugs.

Buddha teaches us to observe reality. Every addiction will be undone if we observe the truth of the sensations on the body with this understanding: "*Anicca, anicca*. This is impermanent." Gradually we will learn to stop reacting.

Dhamma is so simple, so scientific, so true—a law of nature applicable to everyone. Whether one is Buddhist, Hindu, Muslim, Christian; whether one is American, Indian, Burmese, Russian or Italian—it makes no difference; a human being is a human being. Dhamma is a pure science of mind, matter, and the interaction between the two. Do not allow it to become a sectarian or philosophical belief. This will be of no help.

The greatest scientist produced by the world worked to find the truth about the relationship between mind and matter. And discovering this truth, he found a way to go beyond mind and matter. He explored reality not just for the sake of satisfying his curiosity but to find a way to be free of suffering. So much misery in every family, in every society, in every nation, in the entire world. The Enlightened One found a way to come out of this misery.

There is no other solution: each one must come out of misery oneself. When every member of a family comes out of misery, the family will become happy, peaceful and harmonious. When every member of society comes out of misery, when every member of a nation comes out of misery, when every citizen of the world comes out of misery—only then will there be world peace.

There cannot be world peace just because we want world peace: "There should be peace in the world because I am agitating for it." This does not happen. We cannot agitate for peace. When we become agitated, we lose our peacefulness. Let there be no agitation. Purify your mind. Then every action you take will add peace to the universe.

Purify your mind: this is how you can stop harming others and start helping them. When you work for your own liberation, you will find that you have also started helping others come out of their misery. One individual becomes several individuals—there is a slow widening of the circle. But there is no magic, no miracle. Work for your own peace, and you will find that you have started helping the atmosphere around you to become more peaceful, but only when you work properly.

The biggest miracle is changing the habit pattern of the mind from rolling in misery to freedom from misery. There is no bigger miracle than this. Every step that is taken toward this kind of miracle is a healthy step, a helpful step. Every other apparent miracle is only bondage.

May you all come out of your misery, come out of your bondage. May you all enjoy real peace, real harmony, real happiness.

Freedom from Addiction

The following is the closing address by S. N. Goenka at the Seminar on Vipassana for Relief from Addictions & Better Health, Dhamma Giri, 1989.

Friends, you have all participated in this ten-day Dhamma seminar. This is the practical side of Dhamma. Without this experience of the practical side of Dhamma, the theoretical aspect will not be clear. Of course, it is not expected that in ten days you will have grasped the deeper aspects of Dhamma, but you should have gained at least a rough outline of what the path is, a rough outline of what the law of nature is.

I keep repeating that Dhamma does not mean Buddhist Dhamma, or Hindu Dhamma, or Jain Dhamma, or Muslim or Christian or Parsi Dhamma. Dhamma is Dhamma. And also Buddha is Buddha. Not just one person has become a Buddha. Anyone who gets fully enlightened is a Buddha.

And what is full enlightenment? It is the realization of truth at the ultimate level by direct experience. When someone becomes fully enlightened, that person does not establish a particular sect or a particular religion. He just explains the truth that he has realized himself, the truth that can be realized by one and all, the truth which liberates one from all the misery.

The Buddha proclaimed so clearly that one who understands the law of cause and effect, understands Dhamma, and one who understands Dhamma, understands the law of cause and effect. The law of cause and effect is never sectarian. The law of nature is such that the moment you generate negativity in the mind, the mind influences matter, and this reaction which starts within your material structure makes you feel very agitated, makes you feel very unhappy, very miserable. You may call yourself a Hindu, or a Muslim, or a Christian, or a Jain, or a Buddhist. You may call yourself an Indian, or a Pakistani, or a Sri Lankan, or a Burmese, or an American, or a Russian. But the moment you generate negativity in the mind, the law of nature is such that you are bound to become miserable. Nobody can save you from your misery. If you do not generate negativity in your mind, however, you will notice that you are not miserable. A mind that is free of defilements, a pure mind, is again by nature full of love, full of compassion, full of sympathetic joy and full of equanimity.

If there is a practice, if there is a technique, if there is a path that can change the habit pattern of the mind, and the mind can be made pure by washing away the negativities, the defilements; then one who follows it naturally comes out of misery. One may keep calling oneself by any name, it makes no difference. The law is the law: it is universal.

This is the enlightenment of the Buddha and this is what he taught. The Buddha was never interested in a particular philosophy. Most of the time a philosophy is created by people who play games of imagination, of intellectualization. Philosophies are also created by people who may have experienced just a few steps on the path, and with whatever experience they have gained, they form a philosophy which becomes a blind belief for their followers. And this is how sects are established: based on beliefs which are imaginary, or beliefs which are created by intellectual games, or beliefs which are created by partial experience of the truth. An enlightened person understands all of this. He will never insist that people accept whatever he says because he is a realized person, a fully enlightened person. You must realize the truth for yourselves, and here is a process by which you realize the truth directly. You take steps on the path and whatever you have realized, you accept it: and step by step, with an open mind you keep experiencing deeper truths on the path.

The path is there so keep walking on it. Of course, there are rules which must be observed: not to get involved in any kind of imagination; not to get involved in techniques in which you try to see reality with the colored lenses of your own traditional beliefs. Otherwise the technique will not work.

You just observe the reality from moment to moment, as it is, understanding its nature, its characteristic. The reality of the entire universe outside, however, can be experienced only when it comes in contact with the sense doors of your own body, because only the reality within the framework of the body can be directly experienced. And now you have started experiencing this reality within the framework of the body. As I said, in ten days it is not expected that you become perfect in understanding this natural law. But a student who comes to investigate the truth, and works with an open mind, will at least know what the path of truth realization is.

Within these ten days one becomes convinced that the technique is right: that by proceeding on the path the subtler, finer realities pertaining to mind and matter will be realized—the interaction between mind and matter and how one influences the other; that the whole process has nothing to do with this religion or that religion; that it has nothing to do with this belief or that belief. You have worked like scientists investigating the truth by dividing, dissecting, disintegrating, dissolving and analyzing it, not merely at the intellectual level, but at the experiential level, at the actual level. You have taken a tiny step on the path to understand what this mind is; to understand what this matter is. As you proceed further, the path will lead you to the stage where you can experience the dance of every tiny subatomic particle which makes up the physical structure within the framework of your body, as well as outside in the universe; how the tiniest subatomic particle arises and passes, arises and passes. And as with matter, so with the mind. You keep dividing, dissecting and disintegrating, and the reality about the mind becomes clearer and clearer. A stage will come when you will be able to realize the ultimate truth pertaining to the mind; that it too arises and passes, arises and passes. And a time will come when you will be able to realize the ultimate truth pertaining to the mental contents which arise in the mind, the concomitants which arise along with the mind; that their nature is to also arise and pass away, arise and pass away.

This investigation of truth pertaining to matter, pertaining to mind and pertaining to the mental concomitants, the mental contents, is not merely for the sake of curiosity, but to change your mental habit pattern at the deepest level of the mind. As you keep proceeding you will realize how the mind influences matter, and how matter influences the mind.

Every moment, masses of subatomic particles—*kalāpas*—within the framework of the body, arise and pass away, arise and pass away. How do they arise? The cause becomes clear as you investigate the reality as it is without influence from any past conditioning of philosophical beliefs. The material input, the food that you have taken, becomes a cause for these *kalāpas* to arise. You will also find that *kalāpas* arise and pass away due to the climatic atmosphere around you. You also begin to understand the formation of the mind-matter structure; how matter helps matter to arise and dissolve, arise and dissolve. Similarly you understand how mind helps matter to arise and dissolve. You will also notice that at times matter arises from the mental conditioning of the past—that is, the accumulated *saṅkhāras* of the past, the *karma*. By the practice of Vipassana all of this starts to become clear. In ten days you do not become perfect in this understanding but a beginning is made. At this moment, what type of mind has arisen and what is the content of this mind? The quality of the mind is according to the content of the mind. For example, when a mind full of anger, or a mind full of passion, or a mind full of fear has arisen, you will notice that as it arises it helps to generate these subatomic particles.

When the mind is full of passion, then within this material structure, a particular type of subatomic particles arise and there is a biochemical flow, a secretion, glandular or non-glandular, which starts flowing throughout the body with the stream of the blood or otherwise. This type of biochemical flow, which starts because a mind full of passion has arisen, is called *kāmāsava*.

Now as a very honest scientist, you proceed further, just observing the truth as it is, just observing how the law of nature works. When this secretion of *kāmāsava* starts, as it is the biochemical produced by passion, it influences the next moment of the mind with more passion. Thus this *kāmāsava* turns into *kāma-taṇhā* (craving of passion) at the mental level, which again stimulates *kāmāsava*, a flow of passion at the physical level. One starts influencing the other, starts stimulating the other and the passion keeps on multiplying for minutes together, at times for hours together. The behavior pattern of the mind in generating passion gets strengthened because of the repeated generation of passion.

And not only passion but also fear, anger, hatred, and craving—every type of impurity that comes in the mind—simultaneously generates an *āsava* (a flow). And this *āsava* keeps on stimulating that particular negativity, that particular impurity, resulting in a vicious cycle of suffering. You may call yourself a Hindu, or a Muslim, or a Jain, or a Christian: it makes no difference. The process is such, the law is such, that it is applicable to one and all. There is no discrimination.

Mere intellectual understanding will not help break this cycle, and may even create many difficulties. Your beliefs from a particular tradition may look quite logical, yet those beliefs will create obstacles for you. The intellect has its own limitation. You cannot realize the ultimate truth merely at the intellectual level. The ultimate truth is limitless, infinite, and the intellect is finite. It is only through experience that you are able to realize that which is limitless, infinite. Even those who have accepted this law of nature intellectually are not able to change the behavior pattern of their minds, and as a result they are far away from the realization of the ultimate truth.

This behavior pattern is at the depth of the mind. What is called the unconscious mind is actually not unconscious, as at all times it remains in contact with this body. And with this contact of the body a sensation keeps arising, because every chemical that flows in your body generates a particular type of sensation. You feel a sensation—pleasant, unpleasant or neutral, whatever it is—and with the feeling of this sensation, you keep reacting. At the depth of your mind you keep reacting with craving, with aversion; with craving, with aversion. You keep on generating different types of negativities, different types of impurities, and the process of multiplication continues. You can't stop it because there is such a big barrier between the conscious and the unconscious mind. When you practice Vipassana you break this barrier. Without Vipassana the barrier remains.

At the conscious level of the mind, at the intellectual level of the mind, one may accept the entire theory of Dhamma—of truth, of law, of nature. But still one keeps rolling in misery because one does not realize what is happening at the depth of the mind. By direct experience one can understand this. Vipassana helps. And how does it help? Observing your respiration for a few days, you come to a stage where the mind becomes very sharp and very sensitive. And if you work properly, patiently and persistently, most of you in the first ten days, others in the second ten days, come to a stage where you can feel sensations throughout the body. Sensations are there every moment. Every contact results in a sensation—*Phassa paccayā* vedanā. This isn't a philosophy, it is the scientific truth which can be verified by one and all.

The moment there is a contact, there is bound to be a sensation; and every moment the mind is in contact with matter throughout the physical structure. The deeper level of the mind keeps feeling these sensations and it keeps reacting to them. But on the surface the mind keeps itself busy with outside objects, or it remains involved with games of intellectualization, imagination, or emotion. That is the job of your "tiny mind" (paritta citta), the surface level of the mind. Therefore you do not feel what is happening deep inside, and you do not feel how you are reacting to what is happening at the deeper level of the mind.

By Vipassana, when that barrier is broken, one starts feeling sensations throughout the body, not merely at the surface level but also deep inside; as throughout the entire physical structure there is sensation wherever there is life. And by observing these sensations you start realizing the characteristic of arising and passing, arising and passing. By this understanding you start to change the habit pattern of the mind.

Say, for example, you are feeling a particular sensation which may be due to the food you have taken, which may be due to the atmosphere around you, which may be due to your present mental actions, or which may be due to your old mental reactions that are giving their fruit. Whatever it may be, a sensation is there, and you are trained to observe it with equanimity and not to react to it. But you keep on reacting because of the old habit pattern. You sit for one hour, and initially you may get only a few moments when you do not react, but those few moments are wonderful moments. You have started changing the habit pattern of your mind by observing sensation and understanding its nature of impermanence. This stops the blind habit pattern of reacting to the sensation and multiplying the vicious cycle of misery. Initially in an hour you get a few seconds or a few minutes of not reacting. But eventually, with practice, you reach a stage where throughout the hour you do not react at all. At the deepest level you do not react at all. A deep change is coming in the old habit pattern. The vicious cycle is broken: the chemical process which was manifesting itself as a sensation, and which your mind was reacting to with a particular impurity, a particular defilement for hours together, is now getting a break for a few moments, a few seconds, a few minutes. As this habit pattern becomes weaker, your behavior pattern is changing. You are coming out of your misery.

Again, this is not to be believed because the Buddha said so. It is not to be believed because your teacher says so. It is not to be believed because your intellect says so. You have to experience it yourselves. People coming to these courses have found by their experience that there is a change for the better in their behavior.

When we talk of addiction, it is not merely to alcohol or to drugs, but also to passion, to anger, to fear, to egotism: all these are addictions. All these are addictions to your impurities. And at the intellectual level you understand very well, "Anger is not good for me. It is dangerous. It is so harmful." Yet you are addicted to anger, you keep generating anger. And when the anger is over, you keep repeating, "Oh! I should not have generated anger. I should not have generated anger." Meaningless! The next time some stimulation comes, you again become angry. You are not coming out of it, because you have not been working at the depth of the behavior pattern of your mind. The anger starts because of a particular chemical that has started flowing in your body, and with the interaction of mind and matter— one influencing the other—the anger continues to multiply.

By practicing this technique, you start observing the sensation which has arisen because of the flow of a particular chemical. You do not react to it. That means you do not generate anger at that particular moment. This one moment turns into a few moments, which turn into a few seconds, which turn into a few minutes, and you find that you are not as easily influenced by this flow as you were in the past. You have slowly started coming out of your anger.

People who have come to these courses go back home and apply this technique in their daily life by their morning and evening meditation and by continuing to observe themselves throughout the day and night in different situations; how they react or how they remain equanimous to these situations. The first thing they will try to do is to observe the sensation. Because of the particular situation, maybe a part of the mind has started reacting, but by observing the sensation, their minds become equanimous. Then whatever action they take is an action: it is not a reaction. Action is always positive. It is only when they react that they generate negativity and become miserable. A few moments observing the sensation makes the mind equanimous and then it can act. Life then is full of action instead of reaction.

This practice morning and evening, and making use of this technique in daily life, starts to change the behavior pattern. Those who used to roll in anger for a long time find their anger becomes less. When anger comes it cannot last for a long period, because it is not intense. Similarly, those who are addicted to passion find the passion becomes weaker and weaker. Those who are addicted to fear find the fear becomes weaker and weaker. Different kinds of impurities take different amounts of time to come out of. Whether it takes a long time to come out of them, or a short time, the technique will work provided it is used properly.

Whether you are addicted to craving, or aversion, or hatred, or passion, or fear, the addiction is to a particular sensation that has arisen because of the biochemical flow. This type of matter results in reaction at the mental level, and the reaction at the mental level again turns into this biochemical reaction. When you say that you are addicted, you are actually addicted to the sensation. You are addicted to this flow, the biochemical flow.

The *āsava* (flow) of ignorance is the strongest *āsava*. Of course there is ignorance even when you are reacting with anger or passion or fear; but when you get intoxicated with alcohol or drugs this intoxication multiplies your ignorance. Therefore it takes time to feel sensations, to go to the root of the problem. When you are addicted to liquor, or addicted to drugs, you cannot know the reality of what is happening within the framework of the body. There is darkness in your mind. You cannot understand what is happening inside, what keeps on multiplying inside. We have found that in cases of alcohol addiction, people generally start benefiting more quickly than people who are addicted to drugs. But the way is there for everyone to come out of misery, however addicted they may be, however ignorant they may be. If you keep working patiently and persistently, sooner or later you are bound to reach the stage where you start feeling sensations throughout the body and can observe them objectively. It may take time. In ten days you may only make a slight change in the habit pattern of your mind. It doesn't matter: a beginning is made and if you keep on practicing morning and evening, and take a few more courses, the habit pattern will change at the deepest level of the mind and you will come out of your ignorance, out of your reaction.

We keep advising people who are addicted to tobacco— even ordinary tobacco smoking—that if an urge arises in the mind, not to take the cigarette and start smoking. Wait a little. Just accept the fact that an urge to smoke has arisen in the mind. When this urge arises, along with it there is a sensation in the body. Start observing that sensation, whatever the sensation may be. Do not look for a particular sensation. Any sensation at that time in the body is related to the urge to smoke. And by observing the sensation as impermanent *(anicca)*—it arises, it passes, it arises, it passes and in ten minutes, fifteen minutes, this urge will pass away. This is not a philosophy but the experiential truth.

Similarly for those who are addicted to alcohol or addicted to drugs, when an urge arises, we advise them not to succumb immediately, just wait ten or fifteen minutes, and accept the fact that an urge has arisen and observe whatever sensation is present at that time. And they have found that they are coming out of their addictions. They may not be successful every time, but if they are successful even one time out of ten, a very good beginning is made because the root has started changing. The habit pattern lies at the root of the mind, and the root of the mind is strongly related to the sensations on the body: mind and matter are so interrelated, they keep on influencing each other.

If this law, if this nature, is merely accepted at the intellectual level, or devotional level, the benefit will be minimal—it may inspire you to practice. But the real benefit accrues through the actual practice. It is good that all of you have come and given a trial to this technique for ten days. If you are convinced by this trial—that it is a good path, a scientific path, that no blind faith is involved, no dogma is involved, no conversion from one organized religion to another organized religion is involved, that no gurudom is involved, that no guru will liberate you from your addictions or from your miseries, that you have to work out your own salvation—if in these ten days you are convinced that this is a good path, then I would say that you have been successful. It is a long path, a lifetime job. Even a journey of ten thousand miles must start with the first step. For one who has taken the first step it is possible that one will take the second step, the third step, and like this, step by step, one will reach the final goal of full liberation.

May you all come out of all your addictions. Not merely addiction to drugs or alcohol: the addiction to the mental impurities is stronger than these. It has been with you for so many lives; a very strong behavior pattern, which you have to break to come out of your misery. It is a big job. A big responsibility. And you are not doing it to oblige anybody; not to please any God Almighty, not to please your teacher. You are doing it to oblige yourself; for your own good, for your own benefit, for your own liberation. And the process is such that when you start to benefit from the technique, from the path, you cannot resist helping others. It is then not merely for your own good, for your own benefit, for your own liberation, but also for the good, the benefit and the liberation of so many. So many people are suffering all around: may they all come in contact with pure Dhamma and come out of their misery. May they start enjoying peace and harmony; peace and harmony of the liberated mind, liberated from all the defilements.

The Merits of Dāna

The following is a translation of an article originally published in the September 1995 issue of the Hindi Vipaśhyanā Patrikā.

Let us practice and develop the four *brahmavihārā* (the nature of a *brahmā,* hence sublime or divine state of mind, in which the four pure qualities are present):

—the *brahmavihāra* of infinite *mettā,* (loving kindness)

—the *brahmavihāra* of infinite *karuṇā,* (compassion)

—the *brahmavihāra* of infinite *muditā,* (sympathetic joy)

—the *brahmavihāra* of infinite *upekkhā.* (equanimity)

There is a simple way to practice and develop the four *brahmavihārā*: by the giving of *dāna* that is pure in the past, present, and future, and pure in three ways.

How does *dāna* become pure in the past, present and future? When the mind of the donor is suffused with joy and delight before giving *dāna,* while giving *dāna,* and after giving *dāna,* then the *dāna* becomes pure in the past, present and future.

How does *dāna* become pure in three ways? When the mind of the donor is filled with benevolence; when the recipient is living a life of pure *sīla;* and when the *dāna,* irrespective of amount and value, is earned by one's own labor, honestly and through right livelihood; then the *dāna* is pure in three ways.

Dāna that is pure in the past, present, and future, and pure in three ways is highly beneficial.

How does such *dāna* help to develop the four *brahmavihārā*? When the thing or place or facility that is given as *dāna* is not for a particular person but for the benefit and welfare of all meditators, then this *dāna* helps to develop the four *brahmavihārā*.

The mind of the donor is filled with infinite *mettā* when he thinks—"Because of my *dāna*, countless people are gaining or will gain happiness by getting this wonderful Dhamma."

The mind of the donor is filled with infinite *karuṇā* when he thinks—"Because of this *dāna*, there are so many suffering people in the world who will find a way out of their suffering, get the benefit of Dhamma and find contentment."

The mind of the donor is filled with infinite *muditā* with the thought—"Oh! So many people are getting happiness and contentment through the practice of Dhamma because of my *dāna*."

The mind of the donor is filled with infinite *upekkhā* with the thought—"Whether anyone praises my *dāna* or criticizes it, whether I get success or failure because of this *dāna*, it is of no concern to me. My *dāna* is not for self-eulogy or for success or failure. This *dāna*, given with pure volition, is solely for the benefit of others."

In this way, meditators! The four *brahmavihārā* are developed by giving pure *dāna*.

Meditators! The *brahmavihārā* should be practiced and developed. The practice of the *brahmavihārā* is highly beneficial for us.